MARTIN LUTHER KING, JR.

MARTIN LUTHER KING, JR.

❧

Robert Jakoubek

Senior Consulting Editor
Nathan Irvin Huggins
Director
W.E.B. Du Bois Institute for Afro-American Research
Harvard University

CHELSEA HOUSE PUBLISHERS
New York   Philadelphia

Chelsea House Publishers
Editor-in-Chief   Nancy Toff
Executive Editor   Remmel T. Nunn
Managing Editor   Karyn Gullen Browne
Copy Chief   Juliann Barbato
Picture Editor   Adrian G. Allen
Art Director   Maria Epes
Manufacturing Manager   Gerald Levine

Black Americans of Achievement
Senior Editor   Richard Rennert

Staff for MARTIN LUTHER KING, JR.
Copy Editor   Brian Sookram
Deputy Copy Chief   Nicole Bowen
Editorial Assistant   Navorn Johnson
Picture Researcher   Alan Gottlieb
Assistant Art Director   Loraine Machlin
Designer   Ghila Krajzman
Production Coordinator   Joseph Romano
Cover Illustration   Daniel Mark Duffy

5   7   9   8   6

Library of Congress Cataloging-in-Publication Data

Jakoubek, Robert E.
Martin Luther King, Jr.

(Black Americans of achievement)
Bibliography: p.
Includes index.
Summary: Examines the life of the Baptist minister and
civil rights leader who helped American blacks win many
battles for equal rights.
1. King, Martin Luther, Jr., 1929–1968—Juvenile litera-
ture.   2. Afro-Americans—Biography—Juvenile litera-
ture.   3. Baptists—United States—Clergy—Biography—
Juvenile literature.   4. Afro-Americans—Civil rights—Ju-
venile literature.   5. United States—Race relations—
Juvenile literature. [1. King, Martin Luther, Jr.,
1929–1968.   2. Civil rights workers.   3. Clergy.   4. Afro-
Americans—Biography]
I. Title.   II. Series.
E185.97.K5J35   1989   323'.092   [B]   [92]   89-9704

ISBN 1-55546-597-8
    0-7910-0243-8 (pbk.)

Frontispiece: *King leads thou-*
sands of civil rights demonstrators
on the last leg of their 1965
march in Alabama from Selma to
Montgomery.

CONTENTS

BLACK AMERICANS OF ACHIEVEMENT

RALPH ABERNATHY
civil rights leader

MUHAMMAD ALI
heavyweight champion

RICHARD ALLEN
religious leader and social activist

LOUIS ARMSTRONG
musician

ARTHUR ASHE
tennis great

JOSEPHINE BAKER
entertainer

JAMES BALDWIN
author

BENJAMIN BANNEKER
scientist and mathematician

AMIRI BARAKA
poet and playwright

COUNT BASIE
bandleader and composer

ROMARE BEARDEN
artist

JAMES BECKWOURTH
frontiersman

MARY McLEOD BETHUNE
educator

BLANCHE BRUCE
politician

RALPH BUNCHE
diplomat

GEORGE WASHINGTON CARVER
botanist

CHARLES CHESNUTT
author

BILL COSBY
entertainer

PAUL CUFFE
merchant and abolitionist

FATHER DIVINE
religious leader

FREDERICK DOUGLASS
abolitionist editor

CHARLES DREW
physician

W.E.B. DU BOIS
scholar and activist

PAUL LAURENCE DUNBAR
poet

KATHERINE DUNHAM
dancer and choreographer

MARIAN WRIGHT EDELMAN
civil rights leader and lawyer

DUKE ELLINGTON
bandleader and composer

RALPH ELLISON
author

JULIUS ERVING
basketball great

JAMES FARMER
civil rights leader

ELLA FITZGERALD
singer

MARCUS GARVEY
black-nationalist leader

DIZZY GILLESPIE
musician

PRINCE HALL
social reformer

W. C. HANDY
father of the blues

WILLIAM HASTIE
educator and politician

MATTHEW HENSON
explorer

CHESTER HIMES
author

BILLIE HOLIDAY
singer

JOHN HOPE
educator

LENA HORNE
entertainer

LANGSTON HUGHES
poet

ZORA NEALE HURSTON
author

JESSE JACKSON
civil rights leader and politician

JACK JOHNSON
heavyweight champion

JAMES WELDON JOHNSON
author

SCOTT JOPLIN
composer

BARBARA JORDAN
politician

MARTIN LUTHER KING, JR.
civil rights leader

ALAIN LOCKE
scholar and educator

JOE LOUIS
heavyweight champion

RONALD McNAIR
astronaut

MALCOLM X
militant black leader

THURGOOD MARSHALL
Supreme Court justice

ELIJAH MUHAMMAD
religious leader

JESSE OWENS
champion athlete

CHARLIE PARKER
musician

GORDON PARKS
photographer

SIDNEY POITIER
actor

ADAM CLAYTON POWELL, JR.
political leader

LEONTYNE PRICE
opera singer

A. PHILIP RANDOLPH
labor leader

PAUL ROBESON
singer and actor

JACKIE ROBINSON
baseball great

BILL RUSSELL
basketball great

JOHN RUSSWURM
publisher

SOJOURNER TRUTH
antislavery activist

HARRIET TUBMAN
antislavery activist

NAT TURNER
slave revolt leader

DENMARK VESEY
slave revolt leader

MADAM C. J. WALKER
entrepreneur

BOOKER T. WASHINGTON
educator

HAROLD WASHINGTON
politician

WALTER WHITE
civil rights leader and author

RICHARD WRIGHT
author

INTRODUCTION

Coretta Scott King

BEFORE YOU BEGIN this book, I hope you will ask yourself what the word excellence means to you. I think that it's a question we should all ask, and keep asking as we grow older and change. Because the truest answer to it should never change. When you think of excellence, perhaps you think of success at work; or of becoming wealthy; or meeting the right person, getting married, and having a good family life.

Those important goals are worth striving for, but there is a better way to look at excellence. As Martin Luther King, Jr., said in one of his last sermons, "I want you to be first in love. I want you to be first in moral excellence. I want you to be first in generosity. If you want to be important, wonderful. If you want to be great, wonderful. But recognize that he who is greatest among you shall be your servant."

My husband, Martin Luther King, Jr., knew that the true meaning of achievement is service. When I met him, in 1952, he was already ordained as a Baptist preacher and was working towards a doctoral degree at Boston University. I was studying at the New England Conservatory and dreamed of accomplishments in music. We married a year later, and after I graduated the following year we moved to Montgomery, Alabama. We didn't know it then, but our notions of achievement were about to undergo a dramatic change.

You may have read or heard about what happened next. What began with the boycott of a local bus line grew into a national movement, and by the time he was assassinated in 1968 my husband had fashioned a black movement powerful enough to shatter forever the practice of racial seg-regation. What you may not have read about is where he got his method for resisting injustice without compromising his religious beliefs.

He adopted the strategy of nonviolence from a man of a different race, who lived in a distant country, and even practiced a different religion. The man was Mahatma Gandhi, the great leader of India, who devoted his life to serving humanity in the spirit of love and nonviolence. It was in these principles that Martin discovered his method for social reform. More than anything else, those two principles were the key to his achievements.

The book you are holding tells my husband's story. It describes his childhood in Atlanta, Georgia, his interests as a young adult, his study of theology as a college student, and his work as a minister before he got so deeply involved in the civil rights movement. But this is also the story of that movement itself, for it was Martin who brought to it his unique— and ultimately successful—approach.

I was there when it began, in the winter of 1955. During one of his very first speeches Martin said this: "If you will protest courageously, and yet with dignity and Christian love, when the history books are written in future generations, the historians will have to pause and say, 'There lived a great people—a black people—who injected new meaning and dignity into the veins of civilization.' This is our challenge and our overwhelming responsibility." That was the message he never forgot, even during the darkest of times, and it is one we cannot afford to forget today.

Of course, the history of black men and women in America contains many important messages. Not all of the people in this history had the same ideals, but I think you will find something that all of them have in common. Like Martin Luther King, Jr., they all decided to become "drum majors" and serve humanity. In that principle—whether it was expressed in books, inventions, or song—they found something outside themselves to use as a goal and a guide. Something that showed them a way to serve others, instead of living only for themselves.

Reading the stories of these courageous men and women not only helps us discover the principles that we will use to guide our own lives but also teaches us about our black heritage and about America itself. It is crucial for us to know the heroes and heroines of our history and to realize that the price we paid in our struggle for equality in America was dear. But we must also understand that we have gotten as far as we have partly because America's democratic system and ideals made it possible.

We are still struggling with racism and prejudice. But the great men and women in this series are a tribute to the spirit of our democratic ideals and the system in which they have flourished. And that makes their stories special and worth knowing. ❦

MARTIN
LUTHER
KING, JR.

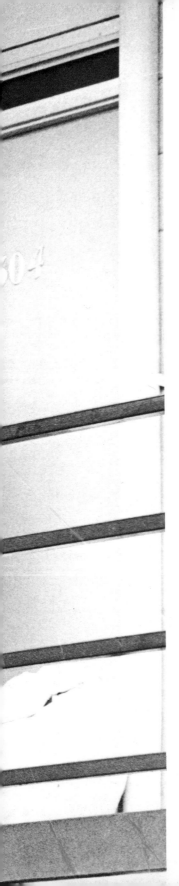

1

APRIL 3, 1968

IT WAS BEFORE dawn when the Reverend Ralph Abernathy brought his old Ford to a stop in front of the modest, pleasant home of Coretta and Martin Luther King, Jr., in Atlanta, Georgia. Abernathy half expected to see King waiting patiently on the stoop, a black valise at his side. But this morning King was running late. When Coretta answered the door, her husband was just getting up.

King mumbled an apology for oversleeping and hurried into the bathroom to shave. Abernathy, after declining Coretta's offer of breakfast, kept a close watch on the time. He and King had to catch an early flight for Memphis, Tennessee.

King was ready in nothing flat. As always, he wore a somber business suit, its well-tailored lines flattering his broad shoulders and subtly concealing his expanding waistline. He gave Coretta a quick good-bye kiss and said he would call her from Memphis. Once in the car, he reminded Abernathy that he wanted to stop by his office on the way to the airport.

When they reached the office on Auburn Avenue, King let himself in with his latchkey and swiftly gathered up some papers he would need in Memphis. In the early morning shadows, an outsider might have

---

King, flanked by his aides Jesse Jackson (left) and Ralph Abernathy, stands on the balcony of the Lorraine Motel shortly after arriving in Memphis, Tennessee, on April 3, 1968. Later in the day, King gave what turned out to be his last public address on civil rights.

taken the place for the office of a law firm or real estate business and King for a young attorney or salesman. Nothing could have been further from the truth.

The office on Auburn Avenue was home to one of the most significant organizations in American history—the Southern Christian Leadership Council (SCLC)—and Martin Luther King, Jr., the man in the dark suit, white shirt, and carefully knotted tie, was its founder and leader. And he had led a revolution.

The revolution of Martin Luther King was the struggle of black Americans for equality and civil rights. For a dozen years, this charismatic Baptist minister and his legion of followers had confronted the humiliating system of segregation that had kept black Americans second-class citizens. In doing this, he and his disciples had faced a raging storm of white abuse. They had been beaten, arrested, jailed, and spat upon. They had had their homes and churches burned, their families threatened, their friends and allies murdered. They had felt the pain of police billy clubs, high-pressure water hoses, and snarling attack dogs. Yet they kept on. They marched; they staged boycotts and sit-ins; they broke unjust laws; and, in the end, they awakened the nation and the world to the shame of American racial persecution.

Through it all, no matter how badly provoked, no matter how brutal their foes, they had never turned to violence, because with every ounce of his being Martin Luther King believed in nonviolence. In accepting one of the world's highest honors, the Nobel Peace Prize, he said, "Nonviolence is the answer to the crucial political and moral questions of our time—the need for man to overcome oppression and violence without resorting to violence and oppression."

During the heroic years of the civil rights movement, Ralph Abernathy had been at King's side, just as he was this morning as they dashed to the Atlanta airport. Others in the movement snickered at the way Abernathy fell asleep during meetings and elbowed his way next to King whenever photographers were around. One associate lamented, "What a burden Ralph was to Martin." Yet King trusted Abernathy absolutely, loved him as a brother, and, despite considerable opposition, had designated him as his eventual successor at the helm of the SCLC.

Abernathy was worried about his loyal friend. A few months before, he had returned from a trip to Europe and had found King dejected and melancholic. "He was just a different person," Abernathy said. "He was sad and depressed." Worst of all, King seemed obsessed by the subject of death and persisted in talking and speculating about his own end.

Those close to King knew he had every reason in the world to be preoccupied with death. As the man who symbolized black America's determination for justice and equality, he magnetically attracted the hatred of violent racists. Over the years, he had received nearly every kind of twisted, anonymous threat of death, and once in New York, a decade before, a deranged woman had stabbed him in the chest as he autographed books in a department store.

The latest reminder of the danger in which King lived took place at the Atlanta airport on this April morning. The scheduled time of departure for Memphis passed, and their plane did not budge. King and Abernathy shifted impatiently in their seats.

Finally, the pilot's voice crackled over the public address system: "Ladies and gentlemen, I want to apologize for the delay. But today we have on board Dr. Martin Luther King, Jr., and we have to be very careful—we had the plane guarded all night—and we have been checking people's luggage. Now that everything's clear, we are preparing for takeoff."

King laughed and shook his head. "In all my flights," he said, "I've never had a pilot say that. If

King returned to Memphis on April 3, 1968, to lead a peaceful march of striking workers that would help boost his Poor People's Campaign, a huge demonstration against poverty. Arriving with him were (from left to right) ministers Andrew Young and Ralph Abernathy and student activist Bernard Lee.

I'm going to be killed it looks like he's trying to make it only too plain to me."

At 10:30 A.M., they landed in Memphis. It was King's third trip to the city in less than three weeks, but it was not a place he particularly wanted to be. He had come to support the city's striking sanitation workers, but every moment in Memphis was one less he had for his principal order of business that spring of 1968: the Poor People's Campaign.

For months, King and the SCLC had been planning a massive demonstration to dramatize the plight of poverty-stricken Americans. It was an ambitious undertaking. King envisioned a great march in Washington, D.C., and the construction in the capital of a "poor people's city" of shacks and shanties that would remain standing until Congress approved sweeping antipoverty legislation. But all sorts of problems threatened to derail the campaign, and to keep it on track King wanted to give it all his time and effort.

Still, the 39-year-old minister could not say no to his friends in Memphis. Overwhelmingly black, the garbage collectors of Memphis were badly paid, overworked, and had no job security, no insurance, no pensions. When it rained, the black workers were sent home without pay, whereas their white supervisors were permitted to wait out the storm and draw their wages.

In February 1968, the garbage collectors went on strike, demanding higher pay and better working conditions and benefits. The local government refused them point-blank, and as the strike dragged on it became a paramount issue for the black community. In March, some black ministers appealed to King. Would he speak at a rally? Reluctantly, he rearranged his schedule, and on March 18 he spoke at Mason Temple. Fifteen thousand people packed the huge old building to hear him speak.

King loved addressing large crowds, and that day he was at the top of his oratorical form. Elated by the cheers, impressed by the sense of commitment in Memphis, he impulsively agreed to head a demonstration for the strikers. "I will lead you on a march through the center of Memphis," he told the crowd.

True to his word, on Thursday, March 28—a hot, uncomfortable day—King was back in town. The march began shortly after 11 o'clock in the morning, with King leading the way, Abernathy and the Memphis ministers at his side, their arms interlocked, their voices raised, singing "We Shall Overcome." Slowly, they moved through the streets toward City Hall, and thousands followed.

They had gotten only a few blocks when everything started to go wrong. Toward the rear of the march, some angry and undisciplined black youths started breaking store windows and looting merchandise. "We can't have that!" King shouted after he heard the sound of glass shattering.

But there was nothing he could do. The march disintegrated into chaos as the youths went on smashing windows and throwing stones and bottles. The Memphis police charged after them, and a full-scale riot was in the making.

On March 28, 1968, King joined forces with co-worker Ralph Jackson (second from left), the Reverend Ralph Abernathy (right), and hundreds of others in Memphis for a demonstration in support of striking laborers. Angry black youths disrupted the march by breaking shop windows and looting the stores, prompting King to set up a second march through the city's streets on April 8.

King himself appeared to be in danger. "You've got to get away from here!" someone yelled at him. Confused and frightened, the group around him pushed forward to Main Street, where King's bodyguard waved a white Pontiac to a stop. "Madam," he said to the black woman behind the wheel, "This is Martin Luther King—we need your car." She consented, and King and Abernathy piled into the backseat. The car then peeled off, racing for a hotel on the other side of town.

By nightfall, a 17-year-old black had been shot dead by the police, 60 of the marchers had been clubbed, and nearly 300 had been arrested. Memphis was declared in a state of emergency. Several thousand National Guardsmen were called in to patrol the streets.

At the Rivermont Holiday Inn, on the banks of the Mississippi, King lay on his bed, the covers pulled up to his chin. He was heartsick. His march had turned into a riot, and the marchers had started it. Had all the years of preaching nonviolence counted for nothing? Were people no longer listening to him? "Maybe we just have to admit that the day of violence is here," he said to Abernathy, "and maybe we have to just give up and let violence take its course. The nation won't listen to our voice—maybe it'll heed the voice of violence."

"It was the most restless night," Abernathy later said. "It was a terrible and horrible experience for him. I had never seen him in all my life so upset and so troubled." Throughout the night, King brooded over the damage done to his movement and to his reputation. His critics, he knew, would have a field day. White conservatives would point to the Memphis fiasco and say that King's nonviolence was a sham. Cautious, moderate blacks would urge him to slow down, to cancel the Poor People's Campaign in Washington. And the militant advocates of Black

Power would proclaim the days of nonviolence and "Martin Loser King" at an end.

Though agonized and in despair that night, King resolved not to give in to his critics or to give up on Memphis. He had to return and lead a peaceful march and demonstration. The Poor People's Campaign depended on it. "If we don't have a peaceful march in Memphis, no Washington," he said. "No Memphis, no Washington."

So, when King arrived in Memphis on April 3, a great deal was at stake. In five days—on Monday, April 8—there was to be another march. This time nothing could go wrong.

Some of the Memphis ministers greeted King at the airport and whisked him off to the Lorraine Motel, in the heart of a black neighborhood, where he checked into room 306, a $13-a-day room with double beds and a view of the parking lot and swimming pool. Almost immediately, he plunged into a long, exhausting series of meetings with the Memphis people and his SCLC associates.

They faced a problem. The city government had obtained an injunction from a federal court prohibiting the march on Monday as a danger to public safety. King decided that the march would proceed, injunction or no injunction. If need be, he would defy a court order. "I am going to lead that march," he said.

Taking a break from the staff meetings, King stepped from his room onto the porch and surveyed the sky. The weather was getting worse. All day there had been tornado warnings; now streaks of lightning flashed, and it started to rain hard.

The bad weather meant that there would not be much of a crowd for a rally that evening at Mason Temple. King had said he would speak there, but he had no desire to address a mostly empty auditorium. What was more, it had been a long day, he had a sore throat, and he was very, very tired. Back inside the room, he appealed to Abernathy, "Ralph, if this rain keeps up, will you go in my place?"

After some hesitation, Abernathy agreed, and around eight o'clock he left the Lorraine for the rally. King changed into his pajamas and settled in for a restful evening by himself.

At 8:30, the phone rang. It was Abernathy. "Martin," he said, "you've got to come over. There's not many people—less than two thousand—but they're so warm, so enthusiastic for you. . . ."

"Well, you don't have to talk that way to me. You know if you say come, I'll come."

King dressed in a hurry and was driven through the rain-swept streets to the temple. It was where he had spoken to a throng of 15,000 in March; this evening less than a seventh of that number awaited him. In soaked clothing, they sat up front. The relentless rain pounded on the building's high tin roof, and the wind seized the shutters at the windows, causing them to slam noisily back and forth. When King entered, the crowd raised a mighty cheer.

Great things were happening in Memphis, he said. Indeed, they were happening all around the world. If God were to give him the chance to live at any time in human history, "I would turn to the Almighty and say, 'If you allow me to live just a few years in the second half of the twentieth century, I will be happy.' " In Africa and Asia, in New York and Atlanta, and now in Memphis, the oppressed had arisen and they cried, "We want to be free." Nonviolence was the way for them. Today, he said, the issue was no longer a choice "between violence and nonviolence—it's nonviolence or nonexistence!"

King thanked God for allowing him to be in Memphis for the march on Monday. Then his voice became softer, more tender, as he recalled the time he had been stabbed in New York in 1958. The blade of the knife had come so close to his heart that a tiny movement, a sneeze even, would have killed him. A girl had written him to say how happy she was that he did not sneeze. "I too am happy I didn't sneeze."

If he had sneezed, he would not have been around for the sit-ins and freedom rides of 1960 and 1961, he said. He would not have seen the blacks of Albany, Georgia, "straighten their backs up" in 1962 as part of a campaign to desegregate the city. If he had sneezed, he would not have been part of the struggle in Birmingham and Selma, and he would never have spoken of his dream for a free and just America at the Lincoln Memorial in 1963. "If I had sneezed," he said, "I wouldn't have been in Memphis to see a great community rally around those brothers and sisters who are suffering.

"I'm so happy that I didn't sneeze."

Outside, bursts of thunder punctuated the hammering of the rain. But no one was paying the storm any mind. Everyone's attention was on the man in the pulpit, whose eyes were watering and whose brow was drenched with sweat, whose next words presaged what would take place on the following day.

King's voice wavered ever so slightly as he revealed the bomb threat on the plane that morning and the warnings against his life in Memphis:

King addresses the congregation at Mason Temple in Memphis on April 3, 1968. Fellow civil rights activists Ralph Abernathy and Andrew Young later noted that King's speech, which marked his last public appearance, ended with a stirring—and ultimately prophetic—allusion to his own death.

But it really doesn't matter with me now, because I've been to the mountaintop. And I don't mind. Like anybody, I would like to live a long life. Longevity has its place. But I'm not concerned about that now. I just want to do God's will. And He's allowed me to go up to the mountain, and I've looked over, and I've seen the promised land. I may not get there with you. But I want you to know tonight, that we, as a people will get to the promised land. And I'm so happy tonight. I'm not worried about anything. I'm not fearing any man. Mine eyes have seen the glory of the coming of the Lord.

2

"YOU ARE SOMEBODY"

❦

MARTIN LUTHER KING, Jr., was born on January 15, 1929, in Atlanta, Georgia, and learned about racial discrimination at an early age. When he was five years old, his most frequent playmate was a white boy whose father owned a neighborhood grocery store. One day, out of the blue, the boy's parents told Martin to go away and not play with their son any longer. Bewildered, Martin asked why. "Because we are white and you are colored," they said.

At home, Martin cried to his mother, "Why don't white people like us?" She dropped everything and for several hours explained the nature of race relations in America, the tragedy of slavery and of segregation. She told him to hold his head high and not let what whites said and did affect him. "You must never feel that you are less than anybody else," she said. "You must always feel that you are *somebody*."

King never really doubted that, but like every southern black, he lived in a segregated, unequal society. "On the one hand, my mother taught me that I should feel a sense of somebodiness," he later explained. "On the other hand, I had to go out and

King (bottom row, fourth from left) at the age of six, attending a birthday party with fellow first graders in his Atlanta neighborhood. "Love was central and . . . lovely relationships were ever present," he later said of his childhood years.

21

face the system, which stared me in the face every day, saying 'You are less than,' 'you are not equal to.' So this was a real tension within."

Throughout the South of King's youth, the system of segregation determined the patterns of life. Blacks attended separate schools from whites, were barred from pools and parks where whites swam and played, from cafés and hotels where whites ate and slept. Blacks never attended major southern universities, and only with the greatest difficulty could they vote in elections. On sidewalks, they were expected to step aside for whites, and if ever a black were to go inside the home of a white, he entered by the back door, never the front. When blacks traveled, they passed through bus and train stations with "colored" waiting rooms, water fountains, and toilets on their way to separate railway coaches or seats at the back of the bus.

It took a brave person to challenge the system. Yet in small ways blacks did their best to resist humiliation. When King was a child, his father took him to buy a pair of shoes at a white-owned store in Atlanta. Father and son took seats in front, near the window. A clerk approached and said, "I'll be happy to wait on you if you'll just move to those seats in the rear of the store."

"Nothing wrong with these seats," the elder King replied.

"Sorry, but you'll have to go back there."

Martin's father stayed put. "We'll buy shoes sitting here or we won't buy shoes at all," he insisted. The clerk shrugged and walked off. In a minute or two, King got up, took Martin by the hand, and strode from the store. On the sidewalk, he looked at his son and in a voice flushed with anger said, "I don't care how long I have to live with this system, I am never going to accept it. I'll oppose it till the day I die!"

Another time young Martin was riding with his father when a policeman pulled them over for a traffic violation. "Boy, show me your license," the officer drawled.

The elder King exploded. Pointing at Martin, he shouted, "Do you see this child here? That's a *boy* there. I'm a *man*. I'm Reverend King."

Indeed he was. The Reverend Martin Luther King, Sr., pastor of the Ebenezer Baptist Church, a leader of black Atlanta, demanded and claimed respect.

In his youth, he had been known as Mike, and he had come up the hard way. Born in 1899, he was from an unhappy family of poor sharecroppers in central Georgia. As a boy, Mike loved church, spent hours studying his Bible, and early on decided to become a minister. "I always felt extremely happy and completely at ease within the church setting," he recalled. "I never tired of going to the revivals, the baptisms, weddings, all the gatherings where people would be found bearing a particular witness."

When Mike reached the age of 15, the deacons of his church licensed him to minister, and he was soon traveling along back roads, preaching the gospel and singing hymns in black churches. Most of his days, however, were spent behind the plow, and he came to hate the tedium of farm work and rural life. After he turned 18, he left home for good, heading for Atlanta.

In the big city, Mike King took one job after another—vulcanizing tires, loading bales of cotton, driving a truck—and in a used Model T Ford that his mother had bought for him by selling a cow, he became something of a man about town. With such a fine car, he remembered, "Nothing I now felt, could stop me. Nothing."

The ministry was still his goal, but country preachers were a dime a dozen in Atlanta. To get

King's father, Martin, Sr., became a preacher at the age of 15 and pastor of Atlanta's well-attended Ebenezer Baptist Church in 1931. Thereafter, church activities played a central role in Martin, Jr.'s life.

ahead, to become the preacher of a leading church, he needed a degree in theology. For an uneducated young man from backcountry Georgia, that was a lot to ask. But Mike's ambition pulled him along. He worked during the day, and at night he studied for a high school diploma. Finally, in 1926, he was admitted to Morehouse College, a respected black school, where he began divinity studies.

Shortly after arriving in Atlanta, Mike King met Alberta Williams, the shy, genteel daughter of one of the city's prominent Baptist ministers. Mike was captivated. Before long, he was the most regular caller at the Williamses' large house on Auburn Avenue. On nice days, the properly chaperoned couple took long rides in Mike's Model T.

During Mike's courtship of Alberta, he won the respect of her father, the Reverend Adam Daniel Williams, pastor of the Ebenezer Baptist Church. The Reverend Williams had risen about as high as a black person could in Atlanta. He ministered to a large congregation, took part in black civic organizations, and was a leading light and charter member of the local chapter of the National Association for the Advancement of Colored People (NAACP), the nation's foremost antidiscrimination organization. Williams let his daughter know that Mike would make a fine husband, and, he added, a fine assistant minister at Ebenezer.

On Thanksgiving Day, 1926, Mike and Alberta were married. They moved in with Alberta's parents, there being plenty of space in the upstairs of the Williamses' 12-room house. Soon, King accepted his father-in-law's offer to become his assistant at Ebenezer, and when Williams died suddenly in 1931, Mike succeeded him in the pastorate.

When the Reverend King first settled in at Ebenezer, old friends still knew him as Mike. But as the years passed, more and more people were calling him

"Daddy," and for the rest of his life that was how he would be best known—as Daddy King. The name fit. Not only was he the fatherly head of a church, but he and Alberta had a family of three splendid children: a daughter, Willie Christine, born in 1927, and two sons, Martin Luther and Alfred Daniel.

Martin Luther King, Jr., arrived in the world at noon on January 15, 1929, in a bedroom of his grandparents' house at 501 Auburn Avenue. Daddy King was so overjoyed at the birth of his first son that he leaped into the air and touched the ceiling. The family quickly took to calling the pudgy, healthy baby "M. L.," and a year and a half later, when a second boy was born, they nicknamed Alfred Daniel "A. D."

Daddy constantly prayed, "God grant my children will not have to come up the way I did." His prayers were answered; the family was well-off. "Not really wealthy," his son Martin would recall, "but Negrowealthy. We never lived in a rented house and we never rode too long in a car on which payment was due, and I never had to leave school to work."

Quite naturally, life revolved around the Ebenezer church. Among M. L.'s earliest memories were the Sunday mornings when his father preached emotional, heartfelt sermons and his mother, the church's musical director, played lovely Christian hymns on the great pipe organ. The King children spent all day Sunday at church, and they were there several afternoons during the week as well. By the time M. L. was five, he was performing gospel songs at church affairs. Accompanied on the piano by his mother, he never tired of singing "I Want to Be More and More Like Jesus."

At home, M. L. was no saint. Once, he clobbered his brother, A. D., over the head with a telephone, knocking him out, and his sister, Christine, could not help but notice how he always seemed to be in the bathroom when it was his turn to do the dishes.

King's mother, Alberta. Her father, the Reverend Adam Daniel Williams, preceded Martin Luther King, Sr., as head of the Ebenezer Baptist Church.

The three children could put aside their squabbling, though not always with a happy result. None of them cared for the piano lessons their mother insisted on, so they conspired against them. A. D. favored a direct approach and started assaulting the living-room piano with a hammer, but M. L. and Christine convinced him to try the more subtle tactic of loosening the legs of the piano stool. Their sabotage went like clockwork: The music teacher arrived, sat on the stool, and crashed to the floor. Had anything, the children

King was born and raised in this house at 501 Auburn Avenue. Located in the heart of black Atlanta, the house stood one block from the Ebenezer Baptist Church.

laughed, ever been so funny? Not in the least amused by the prank, their father gave each of them a thrashing.

It was not the first time M. L. had felt the sting of his father's switch. At home, Daddy meant to be obeyed absolutely. If something went wrong, somebody got a whipping. It was simple, quick, and persuasive, he explained.

"He was the most peculiar child whenever you whipped him," Daddy said of M. L. "He'd stand there, and the tears would run down and he'd never cry. His grandmother couldn't stand to see it." Grandmother Williams, who lived with the Kings, was closest to M. L., and after a spanking, Christine remembered, she always had for him "a hug, kiss, or kind word to help the hurt go away."

M. L. lovingly called her "Mama," and he could not bear the thought of living without her. One day when he was roughhousing with A. D., his brother slid down the banister of the front stairway, missed his mark, and slammed into Mama, knocking her down. When she did not get up, M. L. was sure he and A. D. had killed her. Tears pouring from his eyes, he rushed into a bedroom and threw himself out of a window, landing hard on the ground 12 feet below. When his family hurried to him, shouting that Mama was fine, just a little bruised, M. L. picked himself up and strolled away.

Not long afterward, on a Sunday, M. L. sneaked away to watch a parade—something Daddy had strictly forbidden. When the youngster returned home, the house was filled with sobbing relatives. His grandmother had suffered a heart attack and was dead. Shattered, sensing terrible guilt for having gone to the parade, he once more ran to a second-story window and jumped out. Unhurt beyond some bumps and scrapes, M. L. did not walk away this time. He cried and pounded the ground, a captive of grief.

M. L.'s leaps from upstairs windows naturally concerned his parents. What was he trying to do, they wondered—kill himself? But that seemed unlikely. He never again tried to do himself harm, and in every other way he was a normal, contented youngster. Like most boys, he did neighborhood jobs and delivered newspapers, once saving up $13 of his own. Although always a little small for his age, he enjoyed sports and competed fiercely, especially on the football field, where, said a friend, "he ran over anybody who got in his way." Sometimes, though, he left the playground, usually alone, usually with a book. "Even before he could read he kept books around him, he just liked the idea of having them," Daddy recalled. In school, he was a teacher's dream—smart, disciplined, and well mannered—and he breezed through with such good marks that he skipped grades in elementary school and high school.

By the time M. L. was in his early teens, people commented on how mature he seemed. They took special notice when he spoke. Almost overnight, his voice had changed from a child's chirp into a beautiful, vibrant baritone. Girls his age loved the deep voice and liked the careful way he dressed. In those days, he favored a brown tweed suit, with trousers tight at the ankles and baggy in the legs. Boys, not nearly as impressed, for years called him "Tweed."

At Booker T. Washington High School, M. L. saw his studies suffer a bit because of the time he devoted to romance and dancing. A. D. said of his brother, "I decided I couldn't keep up with him. Especially since he was crazy about dances, and just about the best jitterbug in town."

When M. L. put his mind to it, he could also be the best student in town. When he was 14 and in the 11th grade, he entered an oratorical contest sponsored by a fraternal group, the Negro Elks, and spoke on "The Negro and the Constitution." It was easily the best address, and M. L. won first prize.

The contest was held in Dublin, Georgia—quite a way from Atlanta—and M. L.'s teacher, Mrs. Bradley, accompanied him. On the trip home, the two sat together, talking happily, smiling about the prize-winning day. Then, everything turned to ashes. Twenty years later, King remembered the details vividly:

> Mrs. Bradley and I were on a bus returning to Atlanta, and at a small town along the way, some white passengers boarded the bus, and the white driver ordered us to give the whites our seats. We didn't move quickly enough to suit him, so he began cursing us, calling us "black sons of bitches." I intended to stay right in that seat, but Mrs. Bradley finally urged me up, saying we had to obey the law. And so we stood up in the aisle for the ninety miles to Atlanta. That night will never leave my memory. It was the angriest I have ever been in my life. ❧

3

"I'M GOING TO BE PASTOR OF A CHURCH"

M. L. SAW THE world outside the South for the very first time after his final year in high school, when he took a summer job working in the fields of a Connecticut tobacco farm. Although the work was hard, living in the North gave him, he said, an "exhilarating sense of freedom." When he and his fellow black field hands went into Hartford, they were able to eat in any restaurant, relax in any park, and sit in any seat at a movie theater.

On the train back to Atlanta, M. L. reentered the bitter realm of segregation. He had his choice of seats for the first few hundred miles as the train raced across New York and New Jersey, but by dinnertime the train had reached Virginia. When he went to the dining car, a waiter escorted him to the rear table, and M. L. was asked to pull a curtain around him so whites would not have to see a black man eating. "I felt as though a curtain had dropped on my selfhood," he said.

But slowly, surely, times were changing. In December 1941, when M. L. was 12, the United States had entered World War II, and late in the summer of 1944, as he returned to Atlanta, the struggle was

King (front row, at far left) at the age of 19, attending a lecture at Morehouse College in Atlanta. In class, he was "quiet, introspective, and very much introverted," said one of his professors.

"We loyal Negro American citizens demand the right to work and fight for our country" became the slogan of civil rights activist A. Philip Randolph as he lobbied for black advancement during World War II. A tireless champion of the oppressed, he rose to national prominence after organizing America's first trade union for black workers in 1925.

approaching its climax. Moreover, the war was proving to be a turning point in American racial relations. Defense industries, desperate for labor, offered well-paying assembly-line jobs, and more than a million blacks flocked to factories. There they found themselves, often for the first time, working alongside whites.

The war also inspired a new militancy among black leaders. In 1941, labor organizer A. Philip Randolph prepared to lead a huge march on Washington to protest unfairness in the hiring practices of defense industries. Although many blacks were employed by defense plants, many more remained victims of discrimination and were denied jobs. At the last minute, President Franklin D. Roosevelt prevailed on Randolph to cancel the march. The president agreed to set up a Fair Employment Practices Commission to investigate discrimination against blacks in the war industry.

It was during these days of war and change that King entered college. Because so many 18 and 19 year olds were in the armed forces, Morehouse College in Atlanta offered special admission to high school students. King, only 15, passed the admission exam and in the fall of 1944 took his place in the freshman class.

It had been a foregone conclusion that King would attend Morehouse, an all-male, all-black college and the alma mater of his father and Grandfather Williams. Not so certain, however, was whether he would follow in their footsteps to the ministry. Daddy King envisioned M. L. as his eventual successor at Ebenezer, but M. L. was full of doubts about his father and about his religion. "I had doubts religion was intellectually respectable," he said years later. "I revolted against the emotionalism of Negro religion, the shouting, and the stomping. I didn't understand it and it embarrassed me."

King examined other professions. He considered becoming a doctor, but having little aptitude for science, he chose the law. "I was at that point where I was deeply interested in political matters and social ills," he said, looking back. "I could see the part I could play in breaking down the legal barriers to Negroes."

Sometimes King would stand in front of a mirror in his room at home, pretending to make courtroom speeches to imaginary juries. As it turned out, that was as close as he came to being a lawyer. His years at Morehouse directed him back to his roots, to his family's calling, and he decided to become a Baptist preacher after all. At Morehouse, he discovered a black minister did not have to be fiery and emotional like Daddy King. Instead, he could be like Dr. Benjamin Mays, the college president.

The tall, distinguished Mays was both a refined intellectual and an active champion of black rights. From the pulpit of the Morehouse chapel he called for the black church to put aside some of its religious fundamentalism and lead the protest for social change. When Mays spoke every Tuesday morning, King followed his every word, scribbling page after page of notes. In Mays he saw his vision of "a real minister"—eloquent, erudite, and committed to improving the lot of black Americans.

King's skepticism about the ministry and religion had nearly vanished by his junior year. Mays and the Morehouse faculty provided models of respectability, and King's classes in theology convinced him Christianity was intellectually defensible. During a course about the Bible, he recalled, "I came to see that behind the legends and myths of the Book were many profound truths one could not escape."

In the summer of 1947, when King was 18, he told his parents he meant to be a minister. Daddy masked his elation by gruffly demanding he prove it

At Morehouse College, King was deeply influenced by school president Benjamin Mays (shown here), who advocated social change during his weekly sermons. Mays's quietly dignified preaching style was quite unlike that of King's father, whose sermons were often thunderous and highly emotional.

by delivering a sermon at Ebenezer. Worshipers nearly filled the church's main sanctuary to hear his trial sermon, and the young man amazed them with his poise and power. "Anybody could see that he was going to make a great preacher right off to start," Daddy King remembered. That night, Daddy dropped to his knees and thanked God for having given him such a son. On February 25, 1948, Martin Luther King, Jr., was ordained a minister and made assistant pastor at Ebenezer.

Yet King's education in theology was just beginning. After graduating from Morehouse, the 19-year-old minister chose to attend the Crozer Seminary in Chester, Pennsylvania. "You're mighty young to go to Crozer," Daddy said, but he had no serious objections and wrote a glowing letter supporting his son's application. Crozer was a fine seminary, but more than scholarship recommended it. Far from Atlanta and his domineering father, Crozer offered King a chance to be his own man, to succeed or fail by himself.

For King, Crozer was a new world. Located a few miles south of Philadelphia along the Delaware River, the seminary enrolled fewer than a hundred students, only a handful of them black. Attending an integrated school for the first time, King was highly sensitive to what whites would think of him. Certain they viewed all blacks as lazy, laughing, sloppy, and tardy, he bent over backward to give the opposite impression. "If I were one minute late to class, I was almost morbidly conscious of it and sure that everyone noticed it," he said. "Rather than be thought of as always laughing, I'm afraid I was grimly serious for a time. I had a tendency to overdress, to keep my room spotless, my shoes perfectly shined and my clothes immaculately pressed." Gradually, he relaxed, discovering that most whites at Crozer accepted him as their equal. For a while, he dated a young white woman, a relationship unthinkable in Atlanta.

There was a limit to the tolerance at Crozer, however. On one occasion, a white student from the South burst into King's room, blamed him for a dormitory prank, and pointed a revolver in his direction. Others intervened and hauled the student away. King let the matter drop, neither pressing charges nor appealing to Crozer's administration, and his calm reaction to the incident won the respect of nearly everyone on campus. By the end of his first year, he was one of the most popular students around.

King was one of the brightest as well. His academic record at Morehouse had been mediocre, but at Crozer he started to shine, nearly always getting A's. As he studied works of theology, he gradually developed a personal philosophy that became the intellectual underpinning of his ministry.

One Sunday, King attended a lecture in Philadelphia by Dr. Mordecai W. Johnson, the president of Howard University. Johnson, who had recently returned from India, spoke about Mahatma Gandhi, the leader of the struggle of the Indian people for independence from Great Britain. Unique among political leaders, Gandhi believed in the power of love and insisted that any action or protest against the British imperialists be peaceful and nonviolent. In 1947, Gandhi, a tiny, simple man who did not eat meat and on occasion wore only a loincloth, saw the struggle won when the British admitted defeat and allowed India its freedom.

"I had heard of Gandhi," King recalled, but he had never given him much thought. Yet as Johnson described the man and his movement, King became intrigued. What he heard, he said, "was so profound and fascinating that I left the meeting and bought a half dozen books on Gandhi's life and works." In Gandhi's teachings, love and nonviolence were wedded to the force of a mass movement dedicated to ending oppression. He never talked of hating or destroying the British. He asked his followers to love

Indian leader Mahatma Gandhi's philosophy of nonviolent resistance ultimately served as the model for King's pacifist approach to social change. King later maintained that prior to reading extensively on Gandhi as part of his theological course work at Crozer Seminary, "I thought the only way we could solve our problem of segregation was an armed revolt."

the enemy as they loved themselves. Through love, he said, the oppressors would be redeemed, and they would see the error of their ways.

King was most attracted to Gandhi's concept of *satyagraha*, or the peaceful defiance of government. In response to continued British rule, Gandhi led boycotts, strikes, and marches, each nonviolent but each protesting the evils of imperialism, and each making it more difficult for the British to govern. King recognized in satyagraha a way for black Americans to break the back of segregation. Certainly there were vast differences between India and the United States, but the technique of active, nonviolent resistance to evil became for King the only moral and peaceful path to liberation.

In June 1951, King finished his studies at Crozer and received his bachelor's degree in divinity. He ranked at the top of his class, gave the valedictory address at the commencement, and won a $1,300 scholarship for further study at a graduate school. He decided to use the scholarship to pursue a Ph.D. and settled on the well-regarded School of Theology at Boston University. Daddy King, though impatient for him to return to Ebenezer, appreciated his son's scholarly ambition and rewarded his accomplishments at Crozer with a new bright green Chevrolet.

Early that fall, King loaded his books and clothes into the Chevy and drove from Atlanta to Boston. He found a pleasant apartment on St. Botolph Street and plunged into the demanding graduate curriculum at Boston University. As at Crozer, he excelled in his studies of philosophy and theology, making a powerful impression on the faculty. His academic adviser remembered him as one of the 5 or 6 best graduate students in his 31 years of teaching at the university.

King did not spend every evening in the library. "He just loved to party, he loved to enjoy life," a friend recalled. King had no trouble meeting attractive young women, although he complained to Mary

Powell, an old friend, that in Boston he missed the particular charm of southern women. Mrs. Powell said she knew just the girl for him and gave him the phone number of a young woman from Alabama: Coretta Scott. That night, he called her and asked for a date.

"He had quite a line," Coretta recalled. It was one he had used before. "You know every Napoleon has his Waterloo," he cooed into the phone. "I'm at my Waterloo, and I'm on my knees." Coretta laughed, and when he suggested having lunch together, she happily accepted.

The next day, stepping into his green Chevy, Coretta hastily sized up King as short and unimpressive. But over a long lunch in a cafeteria on Massachusetts Avenue, she changed her mind. "This young man became increasingly better looking as he talked so strongly and convincingly," she said.

On his side of the table, King was falling head over heels in love. "You have everything I have ever wanted in a wife. There are only four things, and you have them all," he said quietly, listing character, intelligence, personality, and beauty.

Those were the right words. Coming from a large family in Alabama, Coretta Scott had needed more than good luck to make it to Antioch College in

A future King: Coretta Scott (middle row, second from right) with classmates at Antioch College in Ohio, before she went on to study at the New England Conservatory of Music. She had planned to pursue a career as a singer before she met and married King and became an active figure in the civil rights movement.

Ohio and then to the New England Conservatory of Music in Boston, where she was studying voice. Determined to be independent, to have a career as a singer, she resisted the idea of marriage. But as King courted her in the spring, summer, and fall of 1952, she came to love him very much.

Daddy King did what he could to break up the couple. Wanting M. L. at Ebenezer, he insisted his son marry an Atlanta girl from a good solid family. At a tense gathering in Boston just before Christmas 1952, Daddy praised the fine, wonderful women M. L. knew and could marry back home. Coretta heard him out, then looked him straight in the eye. "I have something to offer too, Daddy King" she said.

M. L. kept quiet around Daddy but told his mother that nothing was going to prevent him from marrying Coretta. Daddy finally gave in and offered them his blessing, and on June 18, 1953, on the front lawn of Coretta's parents' house in Marion, Alabama, he conducted their marriage ceremony. The newlyweds went to Atlanta for the summer, and in the fall they returned to Boston, moving into a four-room apartment on Northampton Street.

Like his father, King held a traditional view of marriage. During their courtship, he told Coretta he expected his wife to be a mother and homemaker. He was glad for her to finish her musical studies in Boston, and he was delighted to help out around the house until she graduated, but a singing career for her was out. "I'm supposed to earn enough to take care of you and the family," he said.

Coretta accepted her role. "I always said," she recalled, "that if I had not married a strong man, I would have 'worn the pants.' Martin was such a very strong man, there was never any chance for that to happen."

By late 1953, King was hard at work on his doctoral dissertation, an analysis of the differing views of God advanced by two prominent theologians, Paul

Tillich and Henry Nelson Weiman. There was, however, no need to remain in Boston because his classes
and research were nearly completed. He could write
the dissertation elsewhere.

Several of King's professors encouraged him to
take a teaching job. Staying in the academic world,
living and working at a fine college—this was an
attractive prospect. But for King it was never really
tempting. He meant to preach. "I'm going to be pastor of a church," he told Coretta, "a large Baptist
church in the South. . . . I'm going to live in the
South because that's where I'm needed."

Coretta wished they could stay in the North, at
least for a while longer. Growing up in rural Alabama,
she had seen and felt a much harsher racial prejudice
than her husband had. She lived with vivid, searing
memories of bigoted and violent whites who got angry
about her father's modest success in business and
burned his sawmill to the ground. Martin understood
her feelings, but his destiny, he repeated, was in the
South.

Not in Atlanta, though. Daddy King begged
M. L. to return to Ebenezer, but his son wanted the
freedom of his own church.

In Montgomery, Alabama, the Dexter Avenue
Baptist Church was looking for a new pastor. Around
Christmas in 1953, King preached a sermon there
and was impressed by the refined, respectful congregation. The worshipers liked what they saw and
heard, and in April 1954 the church offered him the
pastorate. He accepted.

By late August, Coretta had graduated from the
conservatory, and King had completed his courses at
Boston University. They stuffed their belongings into
the Chevy and drove south. On September 1, they
reached Montgomery, and in a few weeks they were
in their new home: the church parsonage at 309
South Jackson Street, a white frame house in a quiet,
tree-shaded neighborhood. ☙

*In April 1954, King became pas-
tor of the affluent Dexter Avenue
Baptist Church in Montgomery,
Alabama. He remained there
until January 1960, when he left
Dexter to devote himself more
fully to the civil rights struggle.
"History has thrust something
upon me from which I cannot
turn away," he said in resigning
from his pastorship.*

4

MONTGOMERY

MONTGOMERY, ALABAMA, IN 1954 was as segregated a city as there was in the South. White residents loved calling their home "the cradle of the Confederacy"—in 1861, Montgomery had been the Confederacy's first capital—and they did their best to preserve the ways of white supremacy. Of the city's 120,000 citizens, 48,000 were black, and, inevitably, they got the short end of everything. Most blacks lived in ramshackle houses, often without electricity and running water, located on dirty, unpaved streets. Whites owned nearly all the cars in town; blacks depended on city buses to get about. A municipal law even made it a crime for whites and blacks to play cards or checkers together.

To a newcomer like King, the blacks of Montgomery seemed apathetic, resigned to their fate. But the winds of change were beginning to blow more strongly, even in Alabama. In May 1954, the United States Supreme Court issued a monumental decision. In the case of *Brown v. Board of Education*, the court stated, by unanimous vote, "Separate educational facilities are inherently unequal . . . segregation is a denial of the equal protection of the laws." The court, in one stroke, had cut down a central tenet of southern life: segregating school children by race.

Anyone who hoped the system of separate schools for blacks and whites would disappear peacefully or quickly was to be sadly disappointed. The *Brown* decision infuriated the white South. All over Dixie, a cry arose among whites for "massive resistance" to

King with his wife, Coretta, and daughter Yolanda on the steps of the Dexter Avenue Baptist Church, just down the street from the state capitol, in 1956. His insistence that all church members support civil rights groups, register to vote, and regard their pastor as Dexter's chief authority and policymaker helped pave the way for him to become a leading spokesman for Montgomery's black community.

In May 1954, the U.S. Supreme Court ruled in the case of Brown v. Board of Education *that racial segregation in America's schools is unconstitutional. Shown here, outside the U.S. Supreme Court building, are the National Association for the Advancement of Colored People (NAACP) lawyers who argued the case against segregation: (from left to right) Howard Jenkins, James Nabrit, Spottswood Robinson III, Frank Reeves, Jack Greenburg, Thurgood Marshall, Louis Redding, V. Simpson Tate, and George E. C. Hayes.*

integration, and years would pass before blacks and whites would sit together in a classroom. Ominously, in the aftermath of the *Brown* decision, the ranks of the Ku Klux Klan, a white supremacist group, swelled with those who welcomed the organization's aim to thwart integration by terrorizing blacks.

In Montgomery, as in every other segregated southern city, a minority of blacks had done well for themselves. They were the lawyers and doctors, undertakers and store owners, teachers and accountants who served the black community. Quite a few members of this black middle class in Montgomery worshiped at the Dexter Avenue Baptist Church. It was, in Daddy King's words, "a big-shots church," its congregation generally prosperous, well dressed, and restrained. As a measure of their affluence, they paid their new minister $4,200 a year, the most offered by any black church in town.

The churchgoers received their money's worth. In his first year as pastor, King won the respect and affection of the congregation. Seeing him in the pulpit for the first time, some expressed amazement at his youth. But after hearing a sermon or two, they changed their mind. "Suave, oratorical and persuasive" were the words one worshiper used to describe him, and few disagreed.

In his sermons, King attempted to rouse the church into taking a more active part in resisting segregation. Praising the NAACP, he called for his congregation to join the nation's premier civil rights organization. He also wanted to see his flock at the polls. White officials made it extremely difficult for southern blacks to vote, but King told the congregation at Dexter Avenue that they had a duty to pass literacy tests, pay poll taxes, and overcome all the other obstacles to voting.

Across town, another Baptist preacher watched approvingly as King tried to light a fire under the Dexter Avenue parishioners. The Reverend Ralph David Abernathy of the First Baptist Church shared the newcomer's passion for social justice, and in no time the two were the best of friends. King liked Abernathy's direct, earthy manner, and King's sophistication and learning appealed to Abernathy. Often, the Kings got together with Abernathy and his wife, Juanita, for dinner, conversation, and laughter. The two men had a rich sense of humor and loved amusing one another, so dinner frequently dissolved into sidesplitting laughter as Abernathy, in his slow southern drawl, told joke after joke about country life in Alabama, and King provided hysterical imitations of other preachers. "I declare, you two could be on stage," said a friend.

King laughed easily in 1955. Life was treating him well. In the spring, he finished his doctoral dissertation, and not long afterward Boston University awarded him a Ph.D. Best of all, on November 17, 1955, Coretta gave birth to a girl, Yolanda Denise, whom they called Yoki. The new father could scarcely contain his joy.

Two weeks after Yoki's birth, on Thursday evening, December 1, 1955, a small, neatly dressed black woman in Montgomery left work at quitting time, walked across the street to do some shopping at a pharmacy, and then boarded a bus for the ride home. She took a seat toward the rear, in the row just behind the section marked Whites Only. Holding her packages, she was glad to sit down. After a long day, her feet hurt.

As the bus wound its way through Montgomery, it steadily filled with passengers, and soon every seat was taken. When two white men boarded and paid their fares, the bus driver called over his shoulder for the first row of blacks to move back. After some delay, three blacks rose and stood in the aisle. But Mrs. Rosa Parks, her feet aching, her lap covered with packages, did not budge. The driver shouted, "Look woman, I told you I wanted the seat. Are you going to stand up?"

Gently but firmly, Rosa Parks said, "No," and for that she was arrested and thrown in jail. She had

NAACP member Rosa Parks (second from right) and E. D. Nixon (second from left), a former head of the NAACP's Montgomery chapter, arrive at the Montgomery courthouse in March 1956 to appeal her conviction. Three and a half months earlier, she had refused to give her seat to a white man on a Montgomery bus and was promptly arrested for failing to comply with the city's segregation laws.

defied the law that established not only separate seating for blacks and whites but required blacks to surrender their places if buses were filled.

The next morning, King was working at the Dexter Avenue church when his telephone rang. It was E. D. Nixon, a plainspoken Pullman sleeping-car porter and a leader in the Montgomery NAACP. "We got it," he cried. "We got our case!" He explained to King about Parks's arrest and said that this was what he had been waiting for: an incident that could be used to mount a legal challenge to Montgomery's segregation laws. What was more, Nixon exclaimed, the blacks in town should display their anger by launching a boycott of the city buses.

At that moment, King did not completely share Nixon's enthusiasm. To be sure, he knew how deeply Montgomery blacks resented the buses and how they particularly loathed the business of having to give up their seats, something that was not required in many other southern cities. He knew how bus drivers, all of whom were white, insulted and abused black passengers. But he had doubts about a boycott. Nixon assured him it was the only course of action.

A few minutes later, Abernathy called. He endorsed the planned boycott and asked for his friend's backing. King agreed.

King later observed that the black women of Montgomery lost their fear before the men did. The day after the arrest of Rosa Parks, the Women's Political Council, an organization of black activists, started handing out a leaflet calling for blacks to stay off the buses the following Monday, the day Parks's case would come to trial. "If we do not do something to stop these arrests, they will continue," it read. "The next time it may be you, or your daughter, or your mother. . . . Don't ride the buses to work, to town, to school, or anywhere on Monday."

Over the weekend, volunteers blanketed black neighborhoods with leaflets, black cab firms promised to carry riders for what it cost to ride a bus, and King, Abernathy, and others visited bars and nightclubs to speak in support of the boycott. On Sunday, black churchgoers heard their pastors urge them to stay off the buses. Still, it was anyone's guess what would happen on Monday. A Friday night meeting of black leaders at Dexter Avenue had revealed all sorts of disagreement and personal rivalry. As one dissatisfied participant got up to leave, he whispered to King, "This is going to fizzle out. I'm going."

"I would like to go too, but it's in my church," King said wanly. Given the short notice and all the argument, he thought that if 60 percent of the normal black ridership stayed home on Monday, the boycott would be a great success.

A bus stop was right in front of King's house on South Jackson Street, and very early on Monday morning the minister and his wife waited to see how many people were riding on the 6:00 A.M. bus, the first of the day. "Martin, Martin, come quickly!" Coretta cried. Her husband put down his coffee cup in the kitchen and raced to the front window. He could not believe his eyes. The South Jackson line served more blacks than any in the city, and the early bus was usually packed. "Darling, it's empty!" Coretta said. And so was the next bus. And the next.

His emotions surging, King jumped into his car and cruised about Montgomery. On every line, on every bus, black Montgomerians, nearly to a person, honored the boycott. Some took cabs, some drove with friends, one man rode a mule, and a great many walked. But as King crisscrossed the city, he counted only eight blacks riding on buses.

At nine o'clock that morning, hundreds of blacks crowded about the courthouse for the trial of Rosa Parks. In a matter of minutes, the judge found her guilty of violating a state segregation law and fined her $10 and court costs. She and her attorney appealed the verdict, setting in motion a legal challenge

On April 26, 1956, 5 months into the Montgomery bus boycott, King announces to a mass meeting of 3,000 supporters that the black protest against segregation on the city's buses would continue. Although the bus company had stated three days earlier that it would no longer enforce segregation, the city promised that segregation on the buses would continue.

to segregation. E. D. Nixon had been right; it was the case for which they had been looking.

In the afternoon, the local black leadership met to establish a new organization to direct the boycott. At Abernathy's suggestion, they decided to call the new group the Montgomery Improvement Association, or MIA. After agreeing on a name, they turned to electing a president. In a far corner of the room, Rufus Lincoln, a professor from Alabama State, the city's black university, called, "Mr. President, I would like to nominate Reverend M. L. King for president." No other names were placed in nomination, so King was asked if he accepted. "Well, if you think I can render some service, I will," he replied.

"The action had caught me unawares," King later said. It should have. Only 26 years old and not long in town, he assumed that an older, more established figure would be selected. But being a newcomer worked in his favor; he had not been around long enough to take sides in the feuds that divided the black community. Some in the MIA figured that whites would eventually crush the boycott and its leader. When the movement collapsed, they reasoned, why let it fall on us? Let it bury a youngster who could pick up and leave town. Not everyone, though, was cynical. They admired King's decency, eloquence, and the social activism he preached at Dexter Avenue.

A mass meeting that would determine the future of the boycott was scheduled for 7:00 P.M. at the Holt Street Baptist Church. As the MIA's new leader, King was to give the main address. He had not the slightest notion of what to say. He nearly panicked. All of his sermons were carefully written out, studied, memorized, rehearsed. Now he had but 15 minutes to collect his thoughts before heading out for the meeting. In his study at home, he dropped to his knees and prayed for God to be with him.

The church was filled far beyond its capacity. Outside, thousands clogged the streets, and loud-speakers were set up for them to hear the proceedings. After the others spoke, it was King's turn. He started with a calm description of the arrest of Mrs. Parks. Gradually, his voice grew louder and started to rise and fall in a singsong way. His words got stronger: "There comes a time when people get tired. We are here this evening to say to those who have mistreated us so long, that we are tired. Tired of being segregated and humiliated; tired of being kicked about by the brutal feet of oppression."

King asked that the protest adhere to "the deepest principles of our Christian faith. Love must be our regulating ideal." Above all, "we must not become bitter and end up hating our white brothers." The crowd, 1,000 in the church and 4,000 in the streets outside, cheered and shouted, "Amen," as he ended each phrase, but hushed when he spoke again: "If you will protest courageously, and yet with dignity and Christian love, when the history books are written in future generations, the historians will have to pause and say, 'There lived a great people—a black people—who injected new meaning and dignity into the veins of civilization.' This is our challenge and our overwhelming responsibility."

Then King sat down, emotionally drained. The throng exploded in a prolonged arm-waving, hand-clapping ovation. "It was the most stimulating thing I had ever heard," one person said. As King acknowledged the applause, he realized that his 16-minute address "had evoked more response than any speech or sermon I had ever delivered."

The crowd was so large and enthusiastic that there was no question the boycott would continue. That evening, the blacks of Montgomery endorsed the MIA's three demands of the bus company and municipal government: First, bus drivers must stop insulting black riders. Second, passengers should be seated on a first-come, first-served basis, blacks taking seats from the back of the bus and moving toward the front, whites from the front backward. And third, the bus company must consider hiring black drivers for the routes that had black patronage.

The demands did not in any way call for an end to segregation. If the MIA's plan were adopted, blacks would still sit apart from whites. All told, the MIA's proposals amounted to a request for a more polite system of segregation; and with such a modest agenda, King initially hoped for a speedy settlement. Even the most conservative white, he thought, could go along with them.

He was dead wrong. During the first week of the boycott, King and other blacks met with city officials and representatives of the bus company, who would not give an inch. It did not matter that the MIA's plan preserved segregation. "If we granted the Negroes these demands," said the attorney for the bus company, "they would go about boasting of a victory that they had won over the white people; and this we will not stand for."

King admonished himself for having been so optimistic. He should have known better. But it suddenly dawned on him that he and the MIA had taken on an enormous task. If the whites would not budge, neither could the blacks. That meant a boycott lasting not a few days or weeks, but one stretching into months, and such an undertaking called for coordination and planning.

The most pressing need was alternative transportation—some means to carry blacks from their homes on one side of town to their jobs on the other. On Tuesday, December 13, the MIA inaugurated a carefully organized, wonderfully effective car pool. Using 300 cars loaned by black motorists, volunteer drivers shuttled riders from 48 dispatch stations in the black neighborhoods to 42 drop-off stations in other parts of the city. Cars broke down, drivers sometimes got lost, but day after day the car pool efficiently shuttled riders back and forth.

The boycott and car pool united black Montgomery. Every morning at the crack of dawn, members

The Montgomery bus boycott owed a great measure of its success to an efficiently run car-pool system. Throughout the protest, privately owned vehicles, including this church-operated station wagon, delivered black passengers to their destination.

of the city's black elite—lawyers, doctors, professors—offered rides in their Cadillacs and Lincolns to the working poor. "The so-called 'big Negroes,'" King wrote, "who owned cars and had never ridden the buses came to know the maids and the laborers who rode the buses every day." Blacks—rich and poor—resented segregation, and the boycott enabled people to forget their different stations in life and join hands. They came together at the mass meetings of the MIA, held twice a week, on Mondays and Thursdays, in the black churches.

King was the star attraction. "Had he not been there, many people might have gone back to the buses," said one woman. Night after night, he explained the philosophy of nonviolent protest. At the first few meetings, he spoke in broad terms of Christian love and brotherhood, but after a while he came to talk of Gandhi and of the nonviolent resistance that had freed India. In the crowded, overheated churches of Montgomery, the young minister asked of his followers what Gandhi, years before, in a foreign land, had asked of his: "We must meet the forces of hate with the power of love; we must meet physical force with soul force. Our aim must never be to defeat or humiliate the white man, but to win his friendship and understanding."

The whites of Montgomery were in no mood to be loved. With each day of the boycott, blacks proved themselves resourceful, organized, and determined—precisely the opposite of what the whites had always said they were. And leading them was a preacher with a Ph.D. who talked of love, and of Gandhi, and of philosophers the whites had never heard of. They despised him and the disruption he was causing. As long as Montgomery's blacks stayed off the buses, King was a marked man.

Most upsetting were the anonymous threatening phone calls. One Saturday night, between 30 and 40 snarling whites called the Kings' number. "Listen, nigger," said one. "We've taken all we want from you. Before next week, you'll be sorry you ever came to Montgomery."

It was too much. Late one night, King answered the phone and heard another hate-filled voice call him "nigger" and order him out of town. Deathly afraid, he wandered to the stove and put on a pot of coffee. As he waited for the water to boil, he sat at the kitchen table. He bowed his head and said to the Lord that he could not continue. "I am at the end of my powers. I have nothing left. I can't face it alone." Suddenly, his cares vanished; his fears retreated. "At that moment," King said later, "I experienced the presence of the Divine as I had never experienced Him before." An inner voice said, "Stand up for righteousness, stand up for truth; and God will be at your side forever."

On January 30, 1956, King faced stark terror. It was a Monday, the day for an MIA rally, and that evening he spoke at Abernathy's First Baptist Church. Coretta stayed home with the baby. By 9:30, she had on her bathrobe and was in the living room, visiting with Mary Lucy Williams, a member of the Dexter Avenue congregation.

When a loud thump on the front porch interrupted their conversation, Mrs. Williams leaped to her feet. Coretta calmly said, "It sounds as if someone hit the house. We'd better move to the back." Just as they reached the next room, the floor trembled and a thunderous roar nearly deafened them. The living room was filled with broken glass and foul-smelling smoke.

At the MIA meeting, King noticed people scurrying around the church with worried, even tearful expressions. He looked for Abernathy. "Ralph, what's happened?" Abernathy shook his head. "Ralph, you must tell me."

"Your house has been bombed."

Some friends at the church drove King home, and there he embraced Coretta and Yoki. "Thank God you and the baby are all right," he said. The house was filled with people, even the mayor and commissioner of police offering their condolences.

Outside, South Jackson Street was swarming with people. Word of the bombing had flown through the black neighborhood, shocking and enraging all who heard the news. Some in the crowd, intent on revenge, had guns and knives. King stepped onto what was left of his front porch and told everyone that his wife and daughter were fine. Go home and put away your weapons, he said. More violence would not resolve a thing. "I want you to love our enemies," he urged his listeners. "Be good to them. Love them and let them know you love them." The crowd's anger subsided, and the people soon left.

King and his wife, Coretta, meet with reporters on the steps of the Montgomery County Courthouse before his trial in March 1956 for violating a state law forbidding boycotts. Immediately after his conviction, King told his supporters outside the courthouse, "We will continue to protest in the same spirit of nonviolence and passive resistance, using the weapon of love."

In the hours before daybreak, one more visitor arrived: Daddy King. Hearing of the bombing, he had left Atlanta at once, racing through the night in his big car to Montgomery. Come back home, he pleaded with his son, get out before they kill you. M. L. said he could not desert the MIA. "It's better to be a live dog than a dead lion," Daddy growled. But M. L. would not listen. He and Coretta and their baby were going to stay.

The violence kept on. Two nights later, some sticks of dynamite exploded in front of E. D. Nixon's house. The bombings, however, only intensified support for the MIA. Black Montgomery stayed off the buses.

In February, the city government attempted to break the boycott once and for all by obtaining an indictment against almost 100 MIA members for violating an obscure state law forbidding boycotts. To no one's surprise, King's name was at the top of the list. His was the first case to go before the court.

King's trial began on March 19, 1956, in the county courthouse. More than 500 black supporters tried to press into the small courtroom. Those who managed to find seats wore white crosses with hand-lettering that read "Father, forgive them." In King's defense, witnesses testified about the abusive bus system. They made no difference. Three days later, the judge routinely found King guilty and sentenced him to pay a $500 fine or serve 386 days of hard labor. His attorneys immediately appealed the decision.

Meanwhile, the case testing the constitutionality of Alabama's segregation statutes—the lawsuit that had begun with the arrest of Rosa Parks—was advancing through federal courts. In June, a panel of federal judges struck down the bus segregation laws, but the city of Montgomery appealed the decision to the U.S. Supreme Court. Accordingly, the boycott settled into a prolonged legal test of wills.

As long as the car-pool system ran smoothly, the boycott could continue indefinitely. This simple fact reached the whites in City Hall, and in the fall of 1956 they legally attacked the car pools. In November, the city went to court, seeking an injunction to halt the car pools, saying they were a public nuisance. If the car pools were declared illegal, the boycott was as good as dead.

At a Monday night rally, King did not try to minimize the peril. He asked for faith and hope: "This may well be the darkest hour before the dawn. . . . We must go on with the same faith. We must believe a way will be made out of no way."

The next day, November 13, 1956, King sat in the courtroom with the MIA's attorney as the judge considered the city's move to ban the car pools. "I was faltering in my faith and my courage," King recalled. Then a reporter handed him a slip of paper during a late-morning recess. "Here is the decision you've been waiting for," the man said with a smile. It was a wire service bulletin.

King is cheered by his supporters following his conviction for helping to arrange the Montgomery bus boycott. The trial received national news coverage and gave renewed momentum to the city-wide protest.

> Washington, D.C. (AP)—The United States Supreme Court today affirmed a decision of a special three-judge U.S. District Court in declaring Alabama's state and local laws requiring segregation on buses unconstitutional.

King read the words over and over. It was miraculous. At the very moment the movement in Montgomery looked to be in the deepest trouble, the nation's highest court declared that segregation on buses was illegal. The battle had been won.

A month later, one morning a little before six o'clock, a Montgomery city bus drew up in front of King's house on South Jackson Street. Several people were waiting at the bus stop, among them King, Abernathy, and Parks. King entered first and took a seat in one of the front rows. A white man occupied the spot next to him. ✤

5

"THE NUMBER ONE LEADER"

IN LATE 1957, King and an associate were walking through the Atlanta airport on their way to a flight for Montgomery. Looking for a rest room, King saw two doors, one labeled Men, the other Colored. He went into the one marked Men. The whites inside paid him no attention, but the lavatory's black attendant was deeply upset. "Colored men don't come in here," he said.

When King did not depart, the attendant walked toward him, tapped him on the shoulder, and said, "You go in the colored room across the hall." King ignored him. Finally, he turned to the despairing attendant and asked, "Do you mean that every time you need to go to the bathroom you go out of here and all the way to that other room?"

"Yes, sir. That's the place for colored."

Back in the airport corridor, King told his friend what had happened in the rest room. Shaking his head, the 28-year-old minister said, "That's the way most of the Negroes of Montgomery acted before the boycott."

The boycott changed things, unleashing a powerful sense of pride and accomplishment within the black community. For the first time in anyone's memory, blacks, by themselves, had peacefully, successfully overcome segregation.

It was a landmark victory, but one that had flaws and limits. A ruling by the Supreme Court, after all,

"If anybody had asked me a year ago to head this movement, I tell you very honestly that I would have run a mile to get away from it," King said after the success of the Montgomery bus boycott. "As I became involved, and as people began to derive inspiration from their involvement, I realized that the choice leaves your own hands."

was what saved the day. Without the court's decision, the city probably would have put the car pool out of business and broken the boycott.

Furthermore, the movement that sought to love its enemies had not converted many whites. Instead, white Montgomery remained intolerant and prone to terrorism. Even though the boycott had ended, the violence persisted. Three days after Christmas 1956, white thugs opened fire on buses all over town, and in early January 1957, they firebombed four churches, including Abernathy's.

The violence and bigotry of whites, no matter how extreme, left King's commitment unshaken. Blacks in the South, he explained to a leading northern liberal in 1957, must say to whites, "We will match your capacity to inflict suffering with our capacity to endure suffering. We will meet your physical force with soul force. We will not hate you, but we will not obey your evil laws."

By 1957, King's message was reaching an audience that stretched far beyond Montgomery. The bus boycott had captured national attention and had transformed its leader into a celebrated spokesman for civil rights. Nearly every delivery of the mail to the Dexter Avenue Church contained for King speaking invitations, job offers from churches and universities, and publishers' proposals for books. In February 1957, he gained the ultimate stamp of celebrity: His picture appeared on the cover of *Time* magazine. On the inside pages, readers found a flattering profile of "this scholarly Negro Baptist minister."

Fame never went to King's head, and he declined nearly all of the offers. But one invitation he accepted eagerly. The leaders of the new African nation of Ghana requested he attend its independence day ceremonies. For King, the emergence of independent nations in Africa was immensely important. The struggle of American blacks against segregation, in his view, was part of the worldwide quest of oppressed colonial people for liberation. In Ghana, he met the official American representative, Vice-president Richard M. Nixon. "I'm very glad to meet you here," he told Nixon, "but I want you to come and visit us down in Alabama where we are seeking the same kind of freedom Ghana is celebrating."

Neither Nixon nor President Dwight D. Eisenhower came to Alabama to denounce segregation. But in 1957, there came a glimmer of hope. Early in the year, the Eisenhower administration sent to Congress a civil rights bill, the first of the 20th century. In its original form, the measure provided for a civil rights commission to investigate abuses against blacks and permitted the Department of Justice to intervene on behalf of those whose right to vote was denied by southern officials.

Encouraged, King and other leading blacks decided the time was right for a major public demonstration to encourage congressional approval of the civil rights bill. They organized a Prayer Pilgrimage for Freedom, and on May 17, 1957, a crowd of 25,000 blacks and whites came together before the Lincoln Memorial in Washington, D.C. On the monument's steps, America's preeminent blacks, one after another, rose and spoke: Roy Wilkins, executive secretary of the NAACP; labor leader A. Philip Randolph; New York congressman Adam Clayton Powell, Jr.; former baseball great Jackie Robinson; gospel singer Mahalia Jackson; singer Harry Belafonte. Yet it was the 28-year-old preacher from Montgomery who outshone these luminaries and touched the crowd in a way no one else could. "Give us the ballot," King thundered, "and we will transform the salient misdeeds of bloodthirsty mobs into the abiding good deeds of orderly citizens."

Not long afterward, the *Amsterdam News*, the largest black paper in the country, echoed the sen-

After arriving in Montgomery in February 1956, civil rights activist Bayard Rustin became one of King's chief aides and closest friends. Sharing King's commitment to nonviolence, he was instrumental in establishing the Southern Christian Leadership Conference (SCLC), a coordinating council to advise and stimulate black protest groups throughout the South.

timents of most who had heard and seen King in the nation's capital. Martin Luther King, Jr., the paper said, "emerged from the Prayer Pilgrimage to Washington as the number one leader of sixteen million Negroes in the United States."

Congress eventually approved the Civil Rights Act of 1957, but by the time it passed, southern senators and representatives had succeeded in gutting the sections protecting black voting rights. Though disappointed by the compromises, King supported the measure, telling Vice-president Nixon, "The present bill is far better than no bill at all."

King's rise to international fame upset older, more established blacks who envied his appeal. Roy Wilkins of the NAACP, in particular, disapproved of widespread nonviolent protest, and his relations with King were tense, often unfriendly. One prominent black, however, detected greatness in King and encouraged him to a large destiny: Bayard Rustin, who wrote to King at the time of the Prayer Pilgrimage, "The question of where you move next is more important than any other question Negroes face today."

A leading advocate of nonviolent protest, the tall, strikingly handsome Rustin had come on his own to Montgomery during the bus boycott. In a short time, he became King's friend and trusted adviser. Every time they talked, Rustin urged spreading the principles of the Montgomery boycott to the rest of the South.

King needed little convincing. In his view, organizations such as the NAACP had paid insufficient attention to the plight of the average southern black. He envisioned a new organization to coordinate civil rights activity throughout the South. Like the MIA, it would be dedicated to nonviolent mass protest, and, as in Montgomery, it would operate through local churches—the most stable, influential institutions in the black community.

At meetings in Atlanta and New Orleans in early 1957, King, with Rustin at his side, conferred with leading black clergymen and built a new organization. Several months later, in August, more than a hundred delegates convened at the Holt Street Church in Montgomery and officially named their group the Southern Christian Leadership Conference, or SCLC. From the outset, no one but King had been considered for its presidency. "King *was* the Southern Christian Leadership Conference," a supporter asserted.

Two years earlier, the young minister at Dexter Avenue had often sat hour upon hour in his study, meticulously preparing a single Sunday sermon. Now, with the SCLC, the MIA, speeches, fund-raising, and travel, he hardly had a moment for himself. Whenever he could, he worked on a personal account of the bus boycott that Harper and Brothers in New York had contracted to publish. Harper wanted to put the book out while the story of Montgomery was still fresh and had pestered him relentlessly for the manuscript. At last, in the spring of 1958, King completed the book. Carrying the title *Stride Toward Freedom*, it combined autobiography with a step-by-step story of the boycott.

King's growing reputation did nothing for him in Montgomery. On September 3, 1958, he accompanied Abernathy to the Montgomery courthouse for the preliminary hearing of a case that charged Edward Davis with chasing after Abernathy with a hatchet. Abernathy was slated to testify against Davis and had brought along a lawyer, Fred Gray, to counter Davis's anticipated testimony. When King asked if he could speak with Abernathy's lawyer, a guard exploded. "Boy," he yelled at King, "if you don't get the hell away from here, you will need a lawyer yourself." Two policemen rushed in. One grabbed King's arm and twisted it behind his back. In minutes, they had

King is arrested for loitering at the Montgomery courthouse, just before the Reverend Ralph Abernathy was to testify at a hearing. The police officers, unaware of the identity of their charge, treated King with obvious brutality.

dragged him from the courthouse to the police station, where a desk sergeant snarled, "Put him in the hole." The officers shoved, kicked, and twisted their captive into a cell.

Ten minutes passed. Some ranking officers hurried to King's cell and released him. They had discovered who their prisoner was, and, worse, that a news photographer had snapped pictures of the arm-twisting arrest. The police filed a charge against King for loitering, expecting that he would pay a fine and the matter would be dropped. At his trial a few days later, the judge found him guilty of disobeying the police and ordered him to pay $14 or serve 14 days in jail.

King startled the judge by refusing to pay the fine. "Your honor," he said, "I could not in all good conscience pay a fine for an act that I did not commit and above all for the brutal treatment I did not deserve." King decided that by staying behind bars he would dramatically illustrate the violence inflicted by police on other southern blacks. Officials in Montgomery realized they had blundered by arresting King—it had become national news—and a city commissioner quickly paid the $14 fine out of his own pocket. King was a free man, but from then on, he would not hesitate to go to jail for violating laws that protected segregation.

After King's arrest in Montgomery, a family friend warned him of the pitfalls of prominence. "You must be vigilant indeed," he cautioned the preacher. Danger seemed to be everywhere.

A few weeks later, King visited Harlem, Manhattan's sprawling black neighborhood, to promote *Stride Toward Freedom.* On a Saturday afternoon, he sat in Blumstein's department store on 125th Street, autographing copies of his book and surrounded by admirers. Suddenly, a middle-aged black woman burst through the crowd. "Is this Martin Luther King?" she inquired.

"Yes it is," King said, looking up. Hearing that, the woman reached into her handbag, pulled out a razor-sharp, seven-inch-long Japanese letter opener, and shoved it into King's chest. Amid the crowd's screams, guards and police handcuffed the woman and dragged her off. She was eventually confined to a mental institution. In shock but fully conscious, King did not move. With the blade still protruding from his chest, he was carried to an ambulance and taken to Harlem Hospital.

He was very fortunate. The letter opener had come to rest against his aorta. If the blade had entered his chest a fraction of an inch to the other side, or if he had made a sudden movement, sneezed even, he would have bled to death. A team of surgeons worked over him for hours, then assured his friends outside the operating room that he would live.

By late October, King was at home in Montgomery, taking it easy with Coretta, Yoki, and the newest family member, their son, one-year-old Martin Luther King III. Over the Christmas holidays, feeling

King waits for an ambulance moments after a deranged woman stabbed him with a letter opener at a New York store in September 1958. He later referred to this incident in his speeches whenever he was preoccupied with death.

much better, King decided to make a sentimental journey to India, the land of Gandhi.

In early February 1959, he and Coretta touched down in Bombay and started a month-long tour of the cities and villages of the vast country. In New Delhi, the capital, he said, "To other countries I may go as a tourist, but to India I come as a pilgrim. This is because India means to me Mahatma Gandhi." For four hours, he visited with Prime Minister Jawaharlal Nehru, Gandhi's ally in the struggle for Indian independence. King was impressed by Nehru and the Indian disciples of Gandhi, sensing in them a commitment to ending poverty and discrimination, something he doubted President Eisenhower and most American politicians possessed.

The most pressing business King faced as soon as he returned home was getting the SCLC voter registration campaign, its Crusade for Citizenship, off the ground. The SCLC had established headquarters in Atlanta, and it was nearly impossible for King to have a hand in day-to-day activities if he continued living in Montgomery. To give the SCLC his full attention, he and Coretta made the difficult decision to leave the Dexter Avenue Church, their home for five years. In late November 1959, he offered his resignation and told the congregation of his plans in Atlanta.

On Sunday, January 31, 1960, King concluded his farewell sermon at Dexter Avenue by asking for sustained protest "until every black boy and girl can walk the streets with dignity and honor." Monday, in Greensboro, North Carolina, four black freshmen from North Carolina Agricultural and Technical State University, seeking dignity and honor, sat down at a Woolworth's lunch counter. When no one waited on them, they stayed seated, opened their school books, and studied. Word that the four students had broken the whites-only law flashed across the campus.

The next day, more than two dozen students peacefully occupied the counter at Woolworth's. Within 10 days, the sit-ins had spread throughout North Carolina into Virginia and South Carolina. By the end of the year, some 50,000 people had joined the protest against segregation.

The sit-ins were remarkably effective. The well-mannered black students contrasted vividly with the whites who swarmed into the lunchrooms to denounce, abuse, and sometimes burn the protesters with lighted cigarettes. Bad for business, the sit-ins forced many places to give in; before 1960 was over, 126 southern towns had desegregated their lunch counters.

Sit-ins, organized protests against racial discrimination, became a powerful tactic in the battle against segregated lunch counters in 1960. Scenes such as this one, contrasting the abusive segregationists with the dignified protesters, sent a clear message to the nation and resulted in the desegregation of more than a hundred eating establishments in the South.

The first sit-ins were spontaneous and caught the leading civil rights organizations by surprise. But the young protesters, almost to a person, had in mind the example of Martin Luther King when they shunned violence and stoically withstood the taunts of whites. For his part, King admired their courage and tenacity and gave them his full support. Keep to nonviolence and coordinate your activities, he advised them.

In April 1960, King and the SCLC called a conference of the student leaders at Shaw University in Raleigh, North Carolina. His keynote address was enthusiastically received, as was his counsel to form a permanent student organization. His suggestion that they become a youth division within the SCLC, however, did not go over so well. The students liked their independence, so instead of joining the SCLC, they founded the Student Nonviolent Coordinating Committee, or SNCC. King's feelings might have been a little hurt, but he quickly joined SNCC's advisory board and offered its leaders a temporary office next to his own in Atlanta.

The SCLC was not King's sole responsibility. In returning to Atlanta, he had at last accepted his father's offer and become co-pastor at Ebenezer. Daddy King was delighted to have him back in Atlanta, telling the Ebenezer congregation, "He's not little M. L. anymore, now. He is 'Dr. King' now." He also assured friends that his son was "not coming to cause trouble."

Daddy and other prominent blacks in Atlanta had friendly relations with the city's white leadership and had no wish for an aggressive campaign of Atlanta sit-ins. This was, however, exactly what SNCC had in mind, and, reluctantly defying his father, King sided with the students.

At lunchtime on Wednesday, October 19, 1960, 75 blacks tried to be served in the whites-only restaurants of downtown Atlanta stores. At Rich's department store, King and 35 others were arrested for trespassing after the establishment's Magnolia Room refused to wait on them. The police packed them into paddy wagons, and by nightfall King and the others were in the cells of the Fulton County Jail. Refusing to pay a bond, he pledged to "stay in jail 10 years if necessary."

That was the last thing William Hartsfield, the mayor of Atlanta, wanted. Worried about unfavorable national publicity, Hartsfield worked out a compromise between black leaders and the store owners. At City Hall, he announced the release of all those arrested for trespassing with the promise that he would act as an intermediary in talks involving the students and the merchants.

King behind bars, though, was just what the officials of DeKalb County, Georgia, wanted. Months before, he had been arrested there for driving with an expired license, fined $25, and placed on a year's probation. He forgot about the matter, but county officials had not. Hearing of his trespassing arrest, the DeKalb sheriff contacted Atlanta officials, pointed out that King had violated the terms of his probation, and asked that they turn him over. The Atlanta officials agreed.

On Monday, October 24, after the others arrested at the sit-in had been released, the DeKalb sheriff's deputies picked up King and hustled him off to their jail. The following day, a judge found him guilty of breaking probation and cheerfully sentenced him to four months at hard labor in a state prison. King was awakened in his cell at three the next morning by a voice in the darkness: "Get up, King. Did you hear me, King? Get up and come out here. And bring all your things with you." The jailers slapped him into handcuffs, tightened chains around his ankles, and pushed him into the back of a squad car. They drove for hours, the officers silent about their destination.

At eight o'clock, they pulled into the state prison at Reidsville, where grinning guards outfitted their famous new charge in a white uniform with blue stripes and put him in a cell reserved for violent criminals. By himself, in a penitentiary infamous for its abuse of blacks, in a part of rural Georgia where the Ku Klux Klan thrived, King broke down and cried. Ashamed of his despair, he pulled himself together and decided to make the most of his four months in prison. He wrote to Coretta, asking her to send a long list of books.

Unbeknownst to King, his imprisonment had become a factor in national politics. In October 1960, the presidential race between the Republican nominee, Vice-president Richard M. Nixon, and the Democrat, Senator John F. Kennedy, was entering the homestretch, with the two candidates neck and neck.

Nixon kept quiet. Privately, he said King had gotten a "bum rap." The Republicans had been courting the votes of southern whites, however, and were worried that public support for a civil rights leader would cost them at the polls. Kennedy also did not want to disturb the traditionally Democratic whites in Dixie. Yet several members of his campaign staff had been trying to get King out of jail from the time of his arrest in Atlanta.

When King was sent to Reidsville, Kennedy himself acted. He called Coretta in Atlanta, expressed his concern, and said that she should call him if he could do anything else. More to the point, the candidate's brother and campaign manager, Robert F. Kennedy, telephoned the DeKalb County judge who sentenced King and in bold language expressed his outrage. The next day, the judge reopened King's case and allowed a bond to be posted and the prisoner released.

At a happy Atlanta homecoming, King said he was "deeply indebted to Senator Kennedy." The

Democratic presidential candidate John F. Kennedy (left) meets with the Republican candidate, Richard M. Nixon (right), before their first debate in the 1960 campaign. Although neither candidate was anxious to give King his public support and risk losing the votes of southern whites, Kennedy covertly engineered King's release from Georgia's Reidsville state prison in October 1960.

Democrat's intervention similarly impressed blacks throughout the nation. It was simply not the sort of thing white politicians normally did.

On election day, Kennedy defeated Nixon by a tiny margin. Some observers pointed to the Democrat's large number of votes among blacks as making the difference. Eisenhower went so far as to tell reporters that Kennedy had won because he had made "a couple of phone calls."

King, who never formally endorsed Kennedy's candidacy, was among those who celebrated the victory. Was it really possible, he wondered, that black America had a friend in the White House?

6

"I FEEL
THE NEED OF
BEING FREE NOW!"

In OCTOBER 1961, eight months into his presidency, John F. Kennedy invited King to the White House. Their meeting had been a long time coming. King had wanted to talk about civil rights ever since the election, but the president kept putting him off. Finally, when they were together in the president's study, King pressed for legislation to safeguard black voting rights. He reminded the president that 100 years earlier Abraham Lincoln had worked in the very room where they were sitting. What better way to honor the great man's memory, King asked, than for Kennedy to issue a "second Emancipation Proclamation," declaring all forms of segregation illegal.

When King finished laying out his case, Kennedy replied with a lesson in practical politics. It was a bad time for civil rights legislation, he said. Elected narrowly, he faced strong opposition in Congress, and championing the cause of blacks would cost him the support of southern Democrats. Civil rights would have to wait.

King was disappointed but not surprised. By 1961, surely he realized that it was not in the cards for a president of either party willingly to join the civil

A common sight during the civil rights movement: King joining hands with other clergymen at the end of a meeting to sing "We Shall Overcome." The hymn quickly became the anthem of the movement.

rights movement. Kennedy and virtually every other American political leader would delay and temporize forever unless prodded and pushed. And blacks had but one way to pressure the federal government: Massive protest—the nonviolent direct action of demonstrations and sit-ins—got results. The Freedom Rides of 1961 had shown that.

In December 1960, the U.S. Supreme Court outlawed segregation in railroad stations and bus terminals as well as in the trains and buses that crossed state lines. But the South acted as if it had not heard of the decision and kept its facilities as segregated as ever. James Farmer, the head of a pioneer civil rights organization, the Congress of Racial Equality (CORE), decided to dramatize the South's defiance of the court.

In May 1961, two interracial groups, sponsored by CORE, boarded buses in Washington, D.C., and headed southward. Along the way, the Freedom Riders asserted their constitutional rights by ignoring Whites Only and Colored signs in southern bus stations. King gave them his support and had dinner with some of the riders when they passed through Atlanta. Although it was a CORE operation, the SCLC promised cooperation, even paying for the riders' bus tickets to Alabama.

Through Virginia, the Carolinas, and Georgia, the Freedom Ride proceeded uneventfully. This tranquillity bothered Farmer. "We planned the Freedom Ride with the specific intention of creating a crisis," he recalled. "We were counting on the bigots in the South to do our work for us. We figured that the government would have to respond if we created a situation that was headline news all over the world."

In Alabama, they finally got what they expected. At Anniston, a white mob burned one bus and attacked every Freedom Rider it could lay its hands on. The second bus raced to Birmingham, where the po-

lice told a gang of Ku Klux Klansmen they would not interfere with them for 15 minutes. The Klan, in that quarter hour, went after the riders in its preferred way: with lead pipes, baseball bats, and chains.

The outrageous brutality, as Farmer hoped, forced the federal government to act, and it fell to U.S. attorney general Robert F. Kennedy, the president's brother, to protect the Freedom Riders. He sent several assistants to Birmingham, and over the telephone he told an executive of the Greyhound line, "Somebody better get in that damn bus and get it going and get these people on their way." It got as far as Montgomery. There, howling whites surrounded the terminal, and when the Freedom Ride bus pulled in, they screamed, "Get 'em, get 'em, get 'em," and attacked. Clearly, local law enforcement was incap-

In the spring of 1961, an integrated group of Freedom Riders looked to draw national attention to the issue of discrimination on interstate buses by traveling through the South and inciting white segregationists. The passengers achieved their goal on May 14, after a white mob firebombed their bus outside Anniston, Alabama. Photographs of the incident soon circulated throughout the nation.

able of protecting the Freedom Ride, so Kennedy ordered 500 U.S. marshals to Montgomery to restore order.

King was in Chicago on SCLC business. Hearing of the violence, he flew at once to Montgomery. It was a Sunday evening, and at Abernathy's First Baptist Church a rally was quickly arranged. By early evening, more than a thousand blacks, angry about the violence at the bus station, had gathered to hear King. After being escorted from the airport to the church by 50 marshals, he stepped to the pulpit and called for a full-scale assault on segregation in Alabama. He demanded federal support: "Unless the federal government acts forthrightly in the South to assure every citizen his constitutional rights, we will be plunged into a dark abyss of chaos."

By the time King finished speaking, the "dark abyss of chaos" was right on the church's doorstep. A white mob, growing bigger by the minute, was in an early stage of riot. The federal marshals tried to drive them back by firing canisters of tear gas, but the hoodlums pressed in, hurled rocks through the windows, set fire to a car, and gave every sign they meant to burn down the church. Inside, the crowd prayed and bravely sang hymns.

A few minutes after 10:00 A.M., King went to a basement office and called the attorney general in Washington. He informed Kennedy that the mob was going to burn down the church. Kennedy assured him the marshals, who were reinforced by state troopers and the National Guard, could handle the crowd.

The marshals eventually managed to quell and disperse the mob. But it took them all night. Around five in the morning, the people in the church were escorted home by the marshals and guardsmen.

Later that day, the Freedom Riders decided to continue their journey to Mississippi. They expected King to accompany them, but he declined, pointing out that he was still on probation in Georgia for a traffic violation. His explanation satisfied few of the riders and enraged some. "I would rather have heard King say, 'I'm scared—that's why I'm not going,' " one complained, "I would have had greater respect for him if he said that." When King waved good-bye to the heavily guarded bus as it left Montgomery, the riders felt badly let down.

In Mississippi, the riders were arrested as soon as they arrived in Jackson, the state capital, for using the facilities at the main bus station. Attorney General Kennedy remembered, "My primary interest was that they weren't beaten up. So, I suppose I concurred with the fact that they were going to be arrested."

After the arrests, with the threat of white violence diminished, Kennedy tried to arrange their release. King called from Montgomery and informed the attorney general that "as a matter of conscience and morality" the Freedom Riders would stay in jail. Kennedy was nonplussed. What possible good could be done in a cell? "That is not going to have the slightest effect on what the government is going to do in this field or any other," he said to King.

"Perhaps," King replied, "it would help if students came down here by the hundreds—by the hundreds of thousands."

"The country belongs to you as much as to me," Kennedy said, his voice tense with anger. "You can determine what's best just as well as I can, but don't make statements that sound like a threat. That's not the way to deal with us."

Neither man spoke for a while. King broke the silence by trying to explain the philosophy of non-violent resistance, of their need to dramatize the sufferings of blacks by remaining in jail. He could have saved his breath. Kennedy did not see his point. The riders already had the protection of the federal government, he said curtly.

Anxious to preserve the image of the federal government, U.S. attorney general Robert F. Kennedy was often forced to protect the Freedom Riders from violent white mobs. Accordingly, he kept close track of their journey in May 1961 from Montgomery, Alabama, to Jackson, Mississippi.

Ralph Abernathy (left), treasurer of the Southern Christian Leadership Conference (SCLC), and Wyatt T. Walker, the organization's executive director, examine the remains of a black church in Georgia that had been fire-bombed. Throughout the civil rights movement, white segregationists periodically attacked black institutions in an attempt to intimidate blacks.

Now it was King's turn to raise his voice. "I'm deeply appreciative of what the administration is doing," he said. "I see a ray of hope, but I am different than my father. I feel the need of being free now!"

If Kennedy could not see the utility of King's philosophy, he certainly knew political pressure when he saw it. The Freedom Riders gave the very clear lesson that unless segregated bus stations were eliminated, the disruptions would continue. On May 29, 1961, the attorney general requested that the Interstate Commerce Commission issue regulations ending segregation in bus terminals. Soon, the Whites Only signs started coming down all across the South.

Although King's choice not to join the Freedom Ride harmed his reputation with more militant blacks, the SCLC continued to grow impressively. Skillful fund-raising swelled the organization's treasury, and able, talented blacks, attracted to King and his cause, assumed key staff positions. There was, of course, Ralph Abernathy, King's closest friend, who moved to Atlanta to be closer to SCLC affairs. The organization lacked businesslike order until King made Wyatt T. Walker executive director. A minister who had led desegregation efforts in Virginia, Walker was a hard taskmaster, insisting on discipline in the Atlanta office.

If Walker was outspoken and always in motion, Andrew Young was tranquil and deliberate. In his late twenties, Young was an executive with the National Council of Churches in New York. But as he watched the sit-ins and Freedom Rides, he said, "It really disturbed me that things were happening in the South, and I wasn't there." In September 1961, he pulled up stakes and moved to Atlanta, almost at once becoming a central figure in the SCLC's voter education campaign and a trusted aide to King.

With the SCLC in good shape, King, in 1961, planned to accelerate the voter registration effort, and, as he told his friends, "We will have to carry the struggle more into South Carolina, Mississippi, and Alabama." His next and most severe challenge, however, would happen in none of those places, but somewhere the SCLC had not meant to become involved: Albany, Georgia, a city of 56,000 people, 270 miles from Atlanta.

In the summer of 1961, SNCC had initiated a voter registration campaign in Albany. It had been tough going at first, but the movement gradually picked up strength and the effort expanded into sit-ins against segregated public facilities. By mid-December, 471 blacks were in jail, and the town's black community had formed a loose coalition, the Albany Movement.

On the evening of December 15, 1961, King went to Albany with the intention of making a single, morale-boosting speech. When he entered the Shiloh Baptist Church, everyone arose spontaneously to shout and sing "Free-dom, Free-dom, Free-dom."

This marvelous spirit reminded King of Montgomery during the early days of the bus boycott.

In his speech, King talked about nonviolence and civil rights in words he had used hundreds of times to hundreds of audiences. Yet it did not matter to the people in the Shiloh Church, who responded with intense emotion. "Don't stop now," King cried. "Keep moving. Walk together, children. Don't get weary. There's a great camp meeting coming." When he concluded, the crowd sang verse after verse of the old spiritual that was becoming the anthem of the civil rights movement, "We Shall Overcome."

Elated by the response to his words and hearing that Albany's city government had refused to negotiate an end to local segregation, King decided to stay. Late on Saturday afternoon, December 16, he and Abernathy led 250 blacks on a march from the Shiloh Church to City Hall. When they reached the white section of town, Chief of Police Laurie Pritchett and 100 of his officers were waiting. The marchers refused to disband, so the police, using a minimum of force, arrested all of them for obstructing traffic.

From jail, King proclaimed, "I will not accept bond. If convicted I will refuse to pay the fine. I expect to spend Christmas in jail. I hope thousands will join me."

He was in jail only for the weekend. On Monday, he was told of a settlement between the city and local blacks. Accordingly, he allowed his bond to be posted.

Walking out of jail, King discovered he had been hoodwinked. The agreement, negotiated with just a few Albany blacks, was a sham, committing the city to nothing in the way of desegregation. "I'm sorry I was bailed out," he later admitted. "I didn't understand at the time what was happening. We thought that the victory had been won. When we got out, we discovered it was all a hoax."

The SNCC organizers who had started the whole campaign months before were embittered by King's blunder. Julian Bond, a SNCC leader, complained that King had been "losing for a long time. . . . More Negroes and more white Americans will become disillusioned with him, and find that he after all is only another preacher who can talk well."

Aware of this sort of criticism, King refused to give up on Albany. In February 1962, a court found him and Abernathy guilty of all charges stemming from the December march, and a few months later the judge sentenced them either to pay a $178 fine or spend 45 days in jail. Refusing the easy way out, both men chose imprisonment and the chance to draw attention to the injustice of their arrests.

Once more, they were not in jail for long. Albany's mayor, preferring not to have two martyrs in his jail, secretly ordered their release. King wanted to stay behind bars and protested the "subtle and conniving tactics" used to get him out. Abernathy joked, "I've been thrown out of lots of places in my day, but never before have I been thrown out of a jail."

Outmaneuvered again, King vowed to fight back. He summoned his SCLC staff to Albany and pledged a massive, nonviolent campaign to desegregate the city. He informed a cheering rally that they would "fill up the jails" and "turn Albany upside down." For the time being, he had the backing of thousands of the city's blacks, and waves of demonstrators picketed and sat in at segregated restaurants, stores, and public buildings.

Chief Pritchett took it all in stride. Unlike other southern police, he treated blacks respectfully. He bowed his head when the demonstrators prayed, then politely asked them to disperse. "He about stopped our movement," recalled Walter Fauntroy, a SCLC staffer, "because he was so kind."

King with his wife, Coretta, and their children (from left to right) Martin, Dexter, and Yolanda. A fourth child, Bernice, was born in 1963.

Nothing went right. A federal district judge issued an injunction against all forms of protest in Albany, and King obeyed the injunction and halted the demonstrations. This enraged the young SNCC members, who denounced King for timidity. Another court eventually lifted the injunction, but King's caution had cost him valuable support. Then, when he was out of town, a march broke up in disorder, with blacks hurling rocks and bottles at police. "You see them nonviolent rocks?" Pritchett called to reporters.

Still, King pressed on. In late July, he and Abernathy led another march to City Hall and deliberately got themselves arrested. Thrown into the same cell they had occupied before, King read, did some writing, and with Abernathy sang and listened to the radio. After a week, Coretta came for a visit. She brought along Yoki, three-year-old Marty, and Dexter, a baby born in January. (A fourth child, Bernice, was born in March of the following year.) Pritchett allowed their reunion to take place in a corridor so the children did not have to see their father in a cell.

Unfortunately, King's time in the city jail did nothing for the Albany Movement. When the city released him once more, the protest was in a shambles. Bitter disagreements among the city's blacks ruined the prospect of effective mass demonstrations. In late August, they were suspended, and King returned to Atlanta, with Pritchett boasting, "Albany is just as segregated as ever."

He was right. "Our protest was so vague that we got nothing, and the people were left very depressed and in despair," King lamented. The most he would ever claim for Albany was that "the Negro people there straightened up their bent backs; you can't ride a man's back unless it's bent."

King and the SCLC faced facts after their failure in Albany. Since Montgomery, he had been hoping

to convert his enemies. But in seven years, the strategy had not worked once. Southern whites were, by and large, as hostile to blacks as they had ever been.

If whites could not be converted, King decided, then whites would have to be displayed at their ugliest. That was what worked. The savage beatings handed out to the Freedom Riders had prompted the swift intervention of the federal government; but in Albany, where Pritchett had calmly maintained order, the Kennedy administration had kept its distance. Such a thing could not be allowed to happen again. ❧

King with aide Ralph Abernathy (right) in July 1962, speaking to black youths about nonviolence and civil rights. "The old law of an eye for an eye leaves everybody blind," King was known to tell his listeners.

7

"I HAVE
A DREAM
TODAY!"

HERE WAS ONE place where civil rights would never be killed with kindness. Most every black knew that the meanest city in the South, with perhaps the meanest police in the country, was Birmingham, Alabama. Birmingham was Bull Connor's town. Commissioner of Public Safety T. Eugene "Bull" Connor had for years used fear and force to keep this city of 350,000 people (140,000 of whom were black) rigidly segregated. If the SCLC wished to confront a fortress of white supremacy, Birmingham was the ultimate test.

In late 1962 and early 1963, King and his colleagues decided they wanted such a confrontation. Wyatt T. Walker recalled selecting Birmingham "with the attitude we may not win it, we may lose everything. But we knew that as Birmingham went, so would go the South. And we felt that if we could crack that city, then we could crack any city."

The showdown began on April 3, 1963, when King issued a "Birmingham Manifesto" demanding that public facilities be desegregated and that blacks be hired by local merchants. That same day, 65 blacks

King addresses a crowd of nearly 250,000 civil rights marchers gathered at the Lincoln Memorial in the nation's capital on August 27, 1963. The huge, day-long demonstration concluded as the country's foremost civil rights leader told the audience, "I still have a dream. It is a dream deeply rooted in the American dream."

A member of the Student Nonviolent Coordinating Committee (SNCC), a student movement for nonviolent protest, teaches new recruits the art of civil disobedience. In these training sessions, SNCC members sought to show how to protect oneself during a demonstration in addition to controlling one's temper.

sat in at several downtown department stores. Connor's police arrested and jailed 20 of them.

Each evening, King spoke at a mass meeting in one of the city's black churches, recruiting volunteers to march, to sit in, and to be arrested the next day. "I got on my marching shoes!" he cried one night. "I woke up this morning with my mind stayed on freedom! I ain't going to let nobody turn me around! If the road to freedom leads through the jailhouse, then, turnkey, swing wide the gates!" And every night, scores of people would conquer their uncertainty, rise from their seats, and come forward, offering to enlist in the "nonviolent army."

They were divided into small groups, where SCLC staffers instructed them in the methods of nonviolent protest. Then they were told the target of the following day's protest, usually a store or lunchroom. When they were arrested, the SCLC would bail out the demonstrators and send them back into the streets for further protest. By the end of the first week, 300 blacks had gone to jail.

That was not enough. To his dismay, King discovered tremendous resistance to mass demonstrations from many influential Birmingham blacks, and, as a result, recruiting new demonstrators was difficult. Furthermore, Bull Connor had not lived up to his horrible reputation. During the first week of protest, the police had been restrained when making arrests. The city government had also obtained an injunction from a state court forbidding further demonstrations.

King was at a crossroads. If he obeyed an injunction, as he had in Albany, the movement might be stopped dead in its tracks. But if he led a march and went to jail, he would be unavailable to raise funds, and, at that moment, the SCLC had run out of bail money. In meetings at the Gaston Motel, his Birmingham headquarters, King listened to his colleagues argue back and forth. When he had heard enough, he went off to another room and prayed. Half an hour later, he returned to the group, in a change of clothes. Gone was the business suit. In its place was a pair of denim overalls. "The path is clear to me," he said, "I've got to march. I've got so many people depending on me. I've got to march."

In the early afternoon of April 12, 1963—Good Friday—King and Abernathy headed a column of 50 marchers to City Hall. The police intercepted them, made their arrests, and piled King and the others into paddy wagons. At the Birmingham jail, he faced "the longest, most frustrating and bewildering hours I have lived." The jailers—"unfriendly and unbelievably abusive in their language," he said—threw him into solitary confinement, in a cell without a mattress, pillow, or blanket. For a full day, he was held incommunicado—no visitors, no phone calls.

T. Eugene "Bull" Connor (second from right), the police commissioner of Birmingham, Alabama, leads his officers in a mass arrest of civil rights demonstrators in the spring of 1963. Connor's violent methods for keeping peace shocked the entire nation and prompted King to declare, "The eyes of the world are on Birmingham."

King and the Reverend Ralph Abernathy lead a column of marchers through the streets of Birmingham, Alabama, on April 12, 1963, in a protest against racial segregation. Anticipating that they would be arrested by the police for heading the demonstration, both men had put on denims in preparation for being sent to jail.

On Easter Sunday, at home in Atlanta, a very worried Coretta dialed the telephone number of the White House in Washington. She had been persuaded that a call to the president was the best way to draw attention to the deplorable condition of her husband's confinement. The president was away. But 45 minutes later, Robert Kennedy returned her call. "Bull Connor is very hard to deal with. . . . But I promise you I will look into the situation," the attorney general said. The next afternoon, the president himself called. Kennedy stressed that King was safe, and, he went on, "I have just talked to Birmingham, and your husband will be calling you shortly."

In Birmingham, suddenly polite guards entered King's cell and told him he could call home. On the telephone, he assured Coretta he was "pretty good"

and talked for a moment to Yoki and Marty. He then asked Coretta, "Who did you say called you?"

"Kennedy, the president," she replied.

"Did he call you direct?"

"Yes, and he told me you were going to call in a few minutes—"

"Is that known?"

The SCLC made sure it got known, and, before long, everyone was aware that the president had his eye on Birmingham, Alabama.

The president's display of concern caused the police to ease the conditions of King's confinement, and the 34-year-old civil rights leader put his time to good use. Earlier in the year, eight Birmingham clergymen, all of them white, had issued "An Appeal for Law and Order and Common Sense." It urged blacks to refrain from demonstrations. If you must, they advised blacks, seek change in the courts, not in the streets. In his lonely cell, writing first on the margins of a newspaper and then on yellow legal pads provided by his lawyers, King composed a reply to the ministers.

King's letter from the Birmingham jail chastised southern whites for not obeying the Supreme Court's decision of 1954 that declared segregated schools unconstitutional but defended blacks who broke the laws upholding segregation: "One may well ask, 'How can you advocate breaking some laws and obeying others?' The answer lies in the fact that there are two types of laws: just and unjust. I would be the first to advocate obeying just laws. One has not only a legal but a moral responsibility to obey just laws. Conversely, one has a moral responsibility to disobey unjust laws."

The days of segregation were numbered, King wrote. "Oppressed people cannot remain oppressed forever. The urge for freedom will eventually come. This is what happened to the American Negro.

Something within has reminded him of his birthright of freedom; something without has reminded him that he can gain it."

King's "Letter from Birmingham Jail," 6,400 words long, was published as a pamphlet and as a magazine article and soon had a circulation of nearly a million copies.

On April 20, after 8 days in jail, King and Abernathy posted $300 cash bonds and rejoined their SCLC associates at the Gaston Motel. There, pessimism hung in the air. The movement was falling to pieces. Too few people were volunteering to be arrested. Far from filling the jails, the demonstrations had nearly ceased. "We needed more troops," Wyatt T. Walker recalled. "We had run out of troops. We had scraped the bottom of the barrel of adults who would go. We needed something new."

Reluctantly, King decided to use children as demonstrators. All along, Birmingham's black high school and grade school students had been cheering on the protests and clamoring to become involved, but throughout April the SCLC had turned them down. But now, needing to keep the protest alive, King gave his approval to their participation, saying the children would gain "a sense of their own stake in freedom and justice."

On May 2, more than a thousand youngsters marched. They ranged in age from 6 to 16. The sight of what he called so many "little niggers" infuriated Bull Connor, and he ordered his police to arrest them. The next day, an even larger number marched, and this time Connor ordered his men not only to arrest but to repulse the demonstrators. When the marchers reached Kelly Ingram Park, they met a wall of Birmingham police, scores of firemen with high-pressure water hoses, and, on the leashes of handlers, barking, snarling German shepherd attack dogs. On the fringes of the park, a small crowd of black onlookers shouted abuse at the police and firemen.

Confined to an Alabama jail cell for eight days in April 1963, King composed one of his most passionate arguments for nonviolent resistance, "Letter from Birmingham Jail." "Any law that degrades human personality is unjust," he wrote in the essay. "All segregation statutes are unjust because segregation distorts the soul and damages the personality."

When rocks and bottles came flying from the crowd, Connor turned his forces loose. "I want to see the dogs work," he shouted. "Look at those niggers run!" The firemen switched on their hoses, and blasts of water slammed into the demonstrators, smashing them to the ground, ripping off their clothing, knocking them senseless. The dogs grabbed, clawed, and bit. Drenched and bleeding, the marchers broke ranks and fled.

Through it all, a large contingent of reporters and photographers did their jobs. On the evening television news broadcasts and in the next morning's newspapers, the American public saw and read how the police and fire departments of Birmingham, Alabama, had attacked children. The savage face of southern racism was being revealed.

In Washington, President Kennedy told some visitors that the pictures coming from Birmingham had made him "sick." Robert Kennedy was similarly affected and dispatched Burke Marshall, an assistant attorney general, to Birmingham. Marshall's charge was somehow to get negotiations going between blacks and whites. When he arrived, he found both sides suspicious. The whites refused to deal with King. "They wouldn't talk to anybody that *would* talk with him," Marshall remembered. King, too, wondered about Marshall's intentions. Did the Kennedys merely want the demonstrations stopped, or were they truly interested in a desegregated Birmingham?

Marshall convinced King that desegregation was the administration's goal, and the minister gave him his blessing. The city's white business establishment also came around. They preferred, even cherished, segregation, but violence in the streets was ruining their businesses and demolishing Birmingham's reputation. At Marshall's urging, they sat down with a handful of local black leaders and started bargaining seriously.

Meanwhile, the demonstrations continued with a seemingly inexhaustible supply of young marchers. Chanting "We want freedom! We want freedom!" day after day, they faced Connor's police, fire hoses, and dogs. By May 6, more than 3,000 blacks, most of them young, were in jail. "This is the first time in the history of our struggle that we have been literally able to fill the jails," King proclaimed.

On the afternoon of Tuesday, May 7, Birmingham approached utter chaos. Hundreds of demonstrators divided into small groups, tied up downtown traffic, and staged sit-ins at department stores. Once

more, Connor opened up with the fire hoses. The young marchers, schooled by the SCLC, stayed non-violent. But that afternoon, black bystanders threw rocks at the police, and it seemed, sooner or later, a riot was going to occur.

Fortunately, the white businessmen in town were fed up with Bull Connor and the relentless turmoil. On Friday, May 10, after several days of marathon bargaining sessions, they reached agreement with the black representatives. Their accord realized King's Birmingham Manifesto. Within months, lunch counters, rest rooms, fitting rooms, and drinking fountains in the downtown stores would be desegregated. Also, blacks would be hired for sales positions they had never before been allowed to hold.

King addresses a group of school-children in Birmingham, Alabama. To increase the number of civil rights demonstrators and incite segregationist brutality, he asked the city's black youths to take part in the protest marches.

Schoolchildren in Birmingham, Alabama, are taken into custody by the police after participating in a civil rights demonstration. Southern Christian Leadership Conference (SCLC) officials James Bevel, Wyatt T. Walker, and Andrew Young directed the movements of the young troops.

The diehard segregationists did their best to sabotage the settlement. On Saturday evening, May 11, night-riding whites, most likely members of the Ku Klux Klan, firebombed the home of King's brother, A. D., a Birmingham preacher who had taken an active part in the demonstrations. Luckily, A. D. and his family escaped unhurt.

Minutes later, a second bomb exploded outside room 30 of the Gaston Motel, King's headquarters. King had returned to Atlanta for the weekend. Nevertheless, the bombings triggered a riot. Enraged blacks streamed into the streets yelling, "Let the whole city burn!" A car was overturned and set ablaze. Police were attacked. Bricks flew through store windows.

King raced back to Birmingham and did what he could to ease the wrath in the black neighborhoods. He toured bars and pool halls to plead for nonviolence, explaining to the denizens that "Bull Connor is happy when we use force." In his efforts to preserve the peace, King had the public support of the Kennedy administration.

The day after the riot, the president appeared on national television and praised the accord between the city's blacks and whites. The federal government, he warned, would "not permit it to be sabotaged by a few extremists on either side who think they can defy both the law and the wishes of responsible citizens by inciting or inviting violence." He backed up his words by dispatching federal troops to the Birmingham area. Facing such stern pressure from Washington, a new city government began implementing the planned desegregation.

Starting on May 2, 1963, police in Birmingham, Alabama, ordered their dogs to attack crowds of civil rights demonstrators. In addition, fire fighters employed high-pressure water hoses to repel the protesters.

King's brother, A. D., calls for calm following the bombing of his Birmingham, Alabama, home by white terrorists on the night of May 11, 1963. That same evening, a second bomb was detonated by Ku Klux Klan activists outside the motel room that served as King's Birmingham headquarters.

The message of black determination had reached the White House. On civil rights, recalled an assistant to the president, Kennedy always wanted to stay "one step ahead of the evolving pressures, never to be caught dead in the pressures, never to be caught dead in the water, always to have something new." After Birmingham, that "something new" meant requesting from Congress comprehensive civil rights legislation even though it was politically treacherous. The president had come to understand that black Americans would accept from him nothing less.

On June 11, 1963, the president delivered a nationally televised address that outlined his proposal for legislation barring segregation in public accommodations and schools. He asked whites to consider the plight of the American black: "Who among us would be content to have the color of his skin changed and stand in his place? Who among us would then be content with the counsels of patience and delay?" The time had come "for this nation to fulfill its promise" of freedom for all.

The president's strong, memorable words elated King. "He was really great," he enthused to a friend. But tragedy tarnished the day. Hours after Kennedy spoke, Medgar Evers, an NAACP leader, was shot dead in front of his house in Jackson, Mississippi. "This reveals that we still have a long, long way to go in this nation before we achieve the ideals of decency and brotherhood," King said sadly.

Birmingham, the rising tide of black activism, Kennedy's civil rights bill, and Evers's assassination gave a sense of urgency to a plan that had been in the works since early in the year—a plan for a march on Washington. It grew out of A. Philip Randolph's old vision of a massive, orderly, dignified parade in favor of civil rights through the streets of the national capital. Randolph's march, proposed for 1941, had never come off. There had been King's Prayer Pilgrimage in 1957, but for 1963 a much larger demonstration was envisioned, one that would bring the civil rights movement to the front and center of the public's attention.

Once more, Randolph, now 74, took a leading role. But it was King's friend Bayard Rustin who did the hard organizing. He enlarged the purpose of the march so that it embraced both economic opportunity and civil rights—Jobs and Freedom, the marchers' placards would read—and he cajoled virtually every civil rights leader and organization into participating.

On August 28, 1963, they marched. Nearly 250,000 people—black and white, farmers and machinists, northerners and southerners, a great cross section of the civil rights movement—proceeded from the Washington Monument to the Lincoln Memorial. In the symbolic shadow of Abraham Lincoln, speaker after speaker trooped to the rostrum. By three in the afternoon, the summer sun and the listless speeches had exacted a toll. The crowd was bored, restless. Then the magnificent gospel singer Mahalia Jackson sang the spiritual "I've Been 'Buked and I've Been Scorned," and the small talk and milling about stopped.

The white-haired, ramrod-straight Randolph introduced "the moral leader of the nation," and a quarter million voices hailed Martin Luther King, Jr., the last speaker of the day. "I started out reading the speech," he said later, when "just all of a sudden—the audience was wonderful that day—and all of a sudden this thing came to me that I have used—I'd used it many times before, that thing about 'I have a dream'—and I just felt I wanted to use it here."

To an assembly that stretched as far as he could see, and to a television audience that extended around the world, King said:

> I have a dream that one day on the red hills of Georgia, sons of former slaves and sons of former slave-owners will be able to sit down together at the table of brotherhood. . . .
> I have a dream my four little children will one day live in a nation where they will not be judged by the color of their skin but by the content of their character. I have a dream today!

He dreamed of an Alabama where "little black boys and black girls will be able to join hands with little white boys and white girls as sisters and brothers."

> I have a dream that one day every valley shall be exalted, every hill and mountain shall be made low, the rough places made plain, and the crooked places made straight and the glory of the Lord will be revealed and all flesh shall see it together.

He dreamed of freedom ringing from every mountaintop, even "from every hill and molehill of Mississippi."

And when we allow freedom to ring, when we let it ring from every village and hamlet, from every state and city, we will be able to speed up that day when all of God's children—black men and white men, Jews and Gentiles, Catholics and Protestants—will be able to join hands and to sing in the words of the old Negro spiritual, "Free at last, free at last; thank God Almighty, we are free at last."

The day of King's dream was a long way from being realized.

"Let the nation and the world know the meaning of our numbers," protest organizer A. Philip Randolph said in his opening speech at the March for Jobs and Freedom held in the nation's capital on August 28, 1963. Nearly a quarter million demonstrators participated in what King called an attempt "to arouse the conscience of the nation over the economic plight of the Negro."

Tragedy frequently followed triumph during the civil rights movement. Almost two weeks after the march on Washington, the Sixteenth Street Baptist Church in Birmingham, Alabama, was bombed (above) by white terrorists just as services were about to begin. Funeral services were held a few·days later (opposite page) for the four young women who were killed in the blast.

SUNDAY, SEPTEMBER 15, 1963, was a hot, late-summer day in Birmingham, and the windows of the Sixteenth Street Baptist Church were open to catch what little breeze there was. Before 10 o'clock in the morning, a congregation of 400 black worshipers was moving down the aisles into the pews, chatting with the ushers and with one another. Toward the back of the church, four young girls talked and giggled as they slipped on their choir robes.

Just then, a package of dynamite was tossed through a window. One woman remembered hearing a sound like a great clap of thunder and then seeing an awful, blinding light. An explosion blasted a hole in the side of the church. Amid the rubble of broken furniture and shattered glass and in the stench of bluish smoke lay the lifeless bodies of Denise McNair, 11, and Cynthia Wesley, Carol Robertson, and Addie Mae Collins, all 14—the four girls who, a moment before, had been putting on their robes.

"My God, we're not even safe in church!" sobbed a woman fleeing the devastation. As word of the murderous assault spread, blacks poured into the streets, blindly striking back. The near riot only added to the tragedy; in the disturbances, two more young blacks were killed—one by police, the other by a gang of whites—and a half dozen were injured. King came to Birmingham that evening and walked through the ruined, bloodstained church, fighting to restrain his anger. "Not since the days of the Christians in the catacombs," he said, "has God's house, as a symbol, weathered such an attack as the Negro churches."

Nineteen sixty-three was a violent year. On November 22, King was spending the afternoon at home, half working, half watching television. Shortly before two, a program was interrupted by an appalling announcement. "Corrie," he shouted to his wife, "I just heard that Kennedy has been shot, maybe killed."

Coretta ran to him, and together they waited for a further bulletin. In a little while, there came the blunt news that President John F. Kennedy was dead, assassinated while riding in a motorcade through Dallas, Texas. After a long silence, King said, "I don't think I'm going to live to reach forty."

"Oh, don't say that, Martin," Coretta snapped.

"This is what is going to happen to me also. I keep telling you, this is a sick nation. And I don't think I can survive either."

8

"WE ARE DEMANDING THE BALLOT"

PRESIDENT KENNEDY'S SUCCESSOR, Lyndon B. Johnson, entered the White House burdened with the reputation of being a masterful but devious political wheeler-dealer. For Johnson, someone once said, the shortest distance between two points was a tunnel. A southerner from the hill country of Texas, Johnson as a congressman and a senator had compiled a mixed record on civil rights. In the presidency, though, his doubts and equivocations vanished, and he used his considerable political skill to win congressional approval for Kennedy's civil rights bill. Less than two weeks after Kennedy's assassination, he invited King to Washington and convinced him that he was, King later said, "a man who is deeply committed to help us."

President Johnson was friendly, but across town there was a man who loathed King and everything for which he stood. He was J. Edgar Hoover, the director of the Federal Bureau of Investigation (FBI). Hoover was about the last person anyone would choose for an enemy. For 40 years, he had com-

President Lyndon B. Johnson (seated) signs the Civil Rights Act of 1964 on July 2 as King looks on. Later in the day, the president pointedly told King and other black leaders "that the rights Negroes possessed could now be secured by law, making demonstrations unnecessary and possibly even self-defeating."

manded the nation's premier law enforcement agency, and he wielded enormous power. During the long years of his leadership, the FBI had done great things by capturing killers, kidnappers, and spies. But, by the early 1960s, Hoover had outlived his usefulness. He had an increasingly paranoid obsession with communism and believed the Soviet Union's domestic agents were on the verge of overthrowing American freedom.

Hoover had no sympathy for civil rights and very little for blacks, so he and others at the FBI were almost automatically suspicious of King and his movement. FBI agents began keeping tabs on the minister in 1958. What bothered them most was his association with Stanley Levison, a New York lawyer who had helped launch the SCLC. For years, Levison had backed the activities of the American Communist party and, the FBI maintained, served on the party's secret national committee. King liked Levison and turned to him time after time for advice, particularly on matters of fund-raising.

King and fellow black leaders (from left to right) Roy Wilkins, executive director of the National Association for the Advancement of Colored People (NAACP), James Farmer, national director of the Congress for Racial Equality (CORE), and Whitney Young, executive director of the National Urban League, meet with President Lyndon B. Johnson at the White House on January 17, 1964, to discuss the new president's plans for a war on poverty. King supported Johnson's proposals, acknowledging the need "to bring the standards of the Negro up and bring him into the mainstream of life."

As far as is known, Levison never tried to push King into communism or communism into the SCLC. But Hoover refused to believe this. He preferred treating King as if he were a Communist.

In June 1963, President Kennedy told King how Hoover felt and advised him to avoid trouble by cutting his ties with Levison. King said he would think it over. When, ultimately, he did not abandon Levison, Hoover exploded and demanded that Attorney General Robert Kennedy approve the wiretapping of King's home and office. Kennedy, anxious to appease the director, gave him the go-ahead.

Hoover and the FBI got an earful by bugging not only King's Atlanta telephones but also his hotel rooms. The microphone surveillance did not uncover the slightest evidence of Communists infiltrating the civil rights movement, but it did provide the FBI with intimate knowledge of King's private affairs. The Bureau now had tape recordings of what it called "entertainment"—lively parties hosted by King.

During the spring and summer of 1964, as Hoover tried to spread dirt on King's reputation, Johnson worked to push the civil rights bill through Congress. On July 2, 1964, the president got the votes he needed, and Congress gave final approval to a measure that outlawed segregation in public accommodations, forbade unions and employers from practicing racial discrimination, and authorized withholding federal funds from institutions that continued to discriminate against blacks.

Three hours after the bill crossed its final congressional hurdle, Johnson signed it into law, using 72 pens to make a single inscription of his signature. He then passed out the pens as souvenirs. One of them went to King, who, along with other civil rights leaders and members of Congress, proudly watched the president sign the law that made segregation a federal crime.

J. Edgar Hoover, director of the Federal Bureau of Investigation (FBI), ordered constant surveillance of King's activities after the black leader complained that FBI agents had not fully investigated civil rights complaints in the South. In response to King's charge that no one had been arrested in 1963 for the murder of three civil rights workers in Philadelphia, Mississippi, or the bombing of the Sixteenth Street Baptist Church in Birmingham, Alabama, Hoover called King the nation's "most notorious liar."

That July day, in the East Room of the White House, King was the most famous black there, instantly recognized. At the end of 1963, *Time* magazine had acknowledged his stature, designating him its "Man of the Year." For a man who still lived in a rented house in Atlanta and drove a 1960 Ford with 70,000 miles on the odometer, awards and riches counted for little. He told Stanley Levison that the *Time* honor was nice, but with 200 other plaques and citations, "what's one more?"

There was, however, an award that meant a very great deal, and in October 1964, it was announced in Oslo, Norway, that King had won it: the Nobel Peace Prize. Bestowed by the Norwegian parliament on the individual who had done the most effective work in the interest of international peace, it is widely considered the highest honor in the world. At 35, King was the youngest Nobel recipient in history.

In December, he and Coretta led a large, lively entourage of family and friends to Norway for the award ceremony. Several days after his arrival, he traveled to Oslo University to accept the peace prize from King Olaf V of Norway. King delivered a brief, eloquent acceptance speech that called on the world to reject "revenge, aggression and retaliation."

"Only Martin's family and close staff members knew how depressed he was during the entire Nobel trip," Coretta recalled. J. Edgar Hoover and the FBI counted among his worries. Ironically, the award came at a time when the FBI was finally investigating and undermining the Ku Klux Klan's terrorist activities in the South.

Nevertheless, King's Nobel Peace Prize had sent Hoover into a fury. Privately, he raged that King should have gotten the "top alley cat" award, and to the press the FBI director branded him a "notorious liar . . . one of the lowest characters in the country." To prominent politicians, Hoover provided a collection of smears entitled "Martin Luther King, Jr.: His

Personal Conduct," while the Bureau fueled a whispering campaign that had King involved in financial, political, and sexual transgressions. By mid-1964, King knew the FBI had been eavesdropping on him, and he winced at the thought of what their tape recordings, if made public, might do to his reputation. Returning to Atlanta from Europe, he found out how low the FBI could sink.

In early January 1965, at the SCLC offices, Coretta opened a slim package containing a reel of tape and a letter. The tape, when played, revealed King's voice during a series of embarrassing private moments. The unsigned letter accused him of being a "dissolute, abnormal moral imbecile" and seemed to suggest he should commit suicide: "King, there is only one thing left for you to do. . . . You are done. There is but one way out for you. You better take it before your filthy, abnormal fraudulent self is bared to the nation."

King accepts the 1964 Nobel Peace Prize on December 10 in Oslo, Norway. He considered the award the "foremost of earthly honors" and accepted it on behalf of the entire civil rights movement.

King leaves the office of FBI director J. Edgar Hoover in late 1964. One month later, the FBI threatened to discredit King by publicly releasing a tape recording that captured the black leader during a series of personal—and highly embarrassing—incidents.

When Coretta showed her husband the package, he immediately guessed it was the work of the FBI. "They are out to break me," he dejectedly told a friend. "They are out to get me, harass me, break my spirit." He was absolutely correct. The package was the work of William C. Sullivan, Hoover's right-hand man, and the tape was put together from the Bureau's surveillance of King's hotel rooms. Although distraught, King would not let himself be blackmailed. He bravely played the recording for Coretta and his SCLC associates, not denying that the voice on the tape was his.

The FBI had overplayed its hand with the crude blackmail attempt, but Hoover lost none of his interest in King. The surveillance, bugging, and wiretaps continued. Eventually, King and his SCLC friends were able to joke about how "all life is a recording studio for us," and they laughingly enrolled new members in "the FBI Golden Record Club." But humor provided small comfort from the calculated cruelty of J. Edgar Hoover.

Although the trouble with Hoover's FBI was unnerving, it did not dissuade King from proceeding with the SCLC's most ambitious campaign since Birmingham: a crusade for voting rights. The Civil Rights Act of 1964 dealt a swift, powerful blow to southern segregation, and the schools, theaters, restaurants, and hotels of Dixie finally opened their doors to blacks. But the measure did not effectively eliminate discrimination at the polling place. Across the Deep South, white officials used every trick in the book to intimidate blacks from exercising the franchise. In some places, the Klan and local police used force and terror against blacks who wanted to vote. In others, a literacy test that required blacks to do such things as recite the preamble to the Constitution word for word proved effective.

By the mid-1960s, only 6 percent of voting-age blacks were registered in Mississippi, 19 percent in

Alabama, and 32 percent in Louisiana. The situation was worst in rural sections. In 2 Alabama counties where blacks comprised 80 percent of the population, not a single black was on the voting rolls.

For King, the answer was the intervention of the national government. Send federal officials south to register blacks, he said. When he suggested that to Johnson in a meeting at the White House in late 1964, the president agreed: "Martin, you're right about that. I'm going to do it eventually, but I can't get a voting rights bill through in this session of Congress." It was too soon after the Civil Rights Act, Johnson explained.

King, of course, had heard that sort of thing from presidents before, and, once more, he turned to direct action. For the campaign for voting rights, King and the SCLC selected Selma, Alabama, the seat of Dallas County, where of 15,000 blacks eligible to vote, only 383 had succeeded in registering.

If Bull Connor had drawn the civil rights movement to Birmingham, then Dallas County sheriff Jim Clark was the attraction in Selma. A hefty, blustering six-footer, Sheriff Clark swaggered about town in a garish uniform set off by a gold-braided cap and a hand-tooled leather belt that carried his gun, billy club, and, for difficult criminals, his cattle prod. He commanded a volunteer posse of 200 devoted followers and said the only thing wrong with his job was "all this nigger fuss here of late." It was nothing to worry about, though: "We always get along. You just have to know how to handle them."

For more than a year, Clark had been "handling" a SNCC voter registration drive in Dallas County. "We found out SNCC had been driven out of Selma," recalled Hosea Williams, a senior SCLC organizer. "Jim Clark even sent deputies into churches where people would be having worship service, to see whether they were serving God or whether they were talking civil rights."

Although the SNCC effort had been a bust, many of its members did not want help from King and the SCLC. Young SNCC members had nicknamed King "de Lawd" and resented the way his fame overshadowed their movement. Nevertheless, SNCC chairman John Lewis, a soft-spoken former divinity student who greatly admired King, agreed to cooperate with the SCLC in Selma.

The day after New Year's 1965, King came to Selma and addressed 700 enthusiastic followers at Brown Chapel Methodist Church in the heart of the black community. "We are going to start a march on the ballot boxes by the thousands," he proclaimed. "We must be willing to go to jail by the thousands. We are not asking, we are demanding the ballot."

A little more than 2 weeks later, on January 18, 1965, the Selma campaign began when King and John Lewis conducted a march of 400 blacks to the courthouse, where they hoped to register to vote. Sheriff Clark was on the courthouse steps, but, surprisingly, he seemed restrained, not at all the mad dog everyone expected. He merely directed the marchers into an alley behind the courthouse, where he left them alone. The march soon broke up.

King and his associates worried about Clark's peacefulness. If the sheriff and his deputies did not abuse and arrest disenfranchised blacks, the Selma exercise was next to pointless. Clark had to show his true colors soon, King decided, or the SCLC would transfer the voter registration drive to another Alabama county.

That was music to the ears of the more moderate whites in Selma. Led by the director of public safety, Wilson Baker, they had prevailed on Clark not to rough up the demonstrators. With King on the verge of leaving town, their plan appeared to be working.

But Jim Clark could stand the sight of marching blacks only so long. On Tuesday morning, when a column of unregistered blacks paraded to the court-house, the sheriff blew up. He ordered 60 marchers arrested and personally grabbed a local black busi-nesswoman by the back of her collar and shoved her around. On Wednesday, he gave another demon-stration one minute to break up. When nothing hap-pened, he had everyone arrested. By the end of the day, 226 blacks were in jail and the SCLC had what it wanted. "Jim Clark is another Bull Connor," an organizer said. "We should put him on the staff." The strategy of the moderate whites was in ruins.

Over the next few weeks, crowds of blacks kept on marching to the courthouse. On occasion, a few made it inside and actually filed their names with voting registrars, but their registration papers were usually thrown out on some technicality. And on more days than not they had to confront Jim Clark. During a march led by King, the sheriff scuffled with Annie Lee Cooper, a stout 53-year-old matron. "I wish you would hit me, you scum," she screamed at Clark. He promptly did, swinging his billy club across her head with a whack heard across the street. Press photographers captured the incident with their cam-eras, and hundreds of newspapers carried the picture of an Alabama sheriff clubbing a black woman for the crime of wanting to vote.

By February 1, the time had come for King to go to jail. In the morning, at Brown Chapel, the move-ment's headquarters, he addressed hundreds of sup-porters and then directed a march of 260 to the courthouse. After only a few blocks, Director of Pub-lic Safety Baker arrested the entire group for violating Selma's parade ordinance.

King's arrest and the daily marches were begin-ning to have an impact. Bailed out after five days in custody, he flew to Washington, where he met with administration officials and, after some maneuvering, with the president. This time Johnson did not say

King leads a group of 260 civil rights demonstrators in prayer fol-lowing their arrest for violating a city parade ordinance in Selma, Alabama, on February 1, 1965. Once in jail, King and his aide Ralph Abernathy (center) turned down a meal of ham steak and turnip greens, explaining that they always fasted during their first two days behind bars.

that the political timing was bad. Instead, he assured King that he would be sending voting rights legislation to Congress "very soon."

Meanwhile, Alabama was doing its best to sicken the nation. The day following King's conference with Johnson, Sheriff Clark forced 165 black students who had been demonstrating at the courthouse to go at a fast trot to a lockup 6 miles outside of Selma, his posse of deputies poking and shocking them with electric cattle prods as they jogged. After three miles, with the students dropping from exhaustion and some vomiting on the roadside, Clark permitted them to "escape."

A week later, in neighboring Perry County, an evening march sponsored by the SCLC ended in tragedy. After a contingent of lawmen broke up the march, a state trooper chased 26-year-old Jimmie Lee Jackson and his mother into a small restaurant. As young Jackson tried to protect his mother from the trooper's billy club, the officer shot him in the stomach. Gravely wounded, Jackson was taken to Selma's black hospital, where Colonel Al Lingo, head of the Alabama State Police, came to his bedside and charged him with assault and battery with intent to kill a law officer. A few days later, Jackson was dead; on March 3, King preached at his funeral.

After Jackson's funeral, the SCLC announced that on March 7 King and his followers would begin marching from Selma to Montgomery—a distance of 54 miles—where they would present their grievances about voting rights and police brutality to the governor of Alabama, George C. Wallace. The governor had no intention of letting them come. A onetime Golden Gloves boxing champion, he brought to politics the same cocky combativeness he had shown in the ring. Upon becoming governor in 1963, he had sworn, "Segregation now! Segregation tomorrow! Segregation forever!" and in the two years since, he had emerged as the country's foremost opponent of civil rights.

On March 6, Wallace banned the scheduled march, saying it would disrupt traffic on the highway. Furthermore, he ordered Al Lingo of the state police to stop the marchers "with whatever means are available" if they tried leaving Selma.

Late in the morning on Sunday, March 7, 600 blacks assembled at Brown Chapel, ready to defy Governor Wallace and march to Montgomery. King was not among them. He assumed the state troopers would arrest all the marchers before they got out of Selma, and he saw no reason to return to jail. Therefore, he remained in Atlanta while Hosea Williams of the SCLC and John Lewis of SNCC led the march from the Brown Chapel through the streets of Selma to the Edmund Pettus Bridge, over which Highway 80 crossed the Alabama River on its way to Montgomery.

At one end of the bridge, a squadron of blue-uniformed state troopers waited, Sheriff Clark's mounted posse on their flanks. After the marchers came onto the bridge, the voice of a trooper blasted through a bullhorn: "You have two minutes to turn around and go back to your church!" The marchers held their ground, some by kneeling on the pavement.

John Lewis, chairman of the Student Nonviolent Coordinating Committee (SNCC), is felled by the nightstick of an Alabama state trooper during an abbreviated civil rights march from Selma to Montgomery on March 7, 1965. The troopers' violent intervention just past the Edmund Pettus Bridge became known throughout the nation as "Bloody Sunday."

"Troopers advance!" came the command. With that, the police surged forward, their billy clubs flailing. As the first few blacks were clubbed down, loud cheers and rebel yells went up from a group of approving white bystanders. Into the marchers, now in desperate retreat, rode Clark's posse, their horses spurred to a gallop.

Moments later, an acrid cloud of smoke spread over the chaotic scene. "Tear gas!" shouted a marcher. Protected by gas masks, the troopers pressed ahead into the coughing, blinded throng. "It was like a battle zone: all those people choking in the gas, being hit and beaten," remembered Lewis, himself clubbed by a trooper.

Heeding Clark's command, "Get those goddamn niggers!" the mounted posse chased the defenseless demonstrators all the way back to the Brown Chapel. Nearly 80 marchers were treated for fractured skulls, broken ribs, head gashes, and a dozen other injuries at the local hospital.

In Atlanta, King was horrified by the events of what came to be known as "Bloody Sunday." Experiencing what he called "an agony of conscience" for not having been in Selma, he at once announced his intention of personally leading a second march to Montgomery on Tuesday, March 9, just two days away. To his fellow ministers and to civil rights supporters around the nation, he issued a public appeal: Come to Selma; join us Tuesday in a ministers' march to Montgomery. In impressive numbers, his allies heeded the call, dropped what they were doing, and flew to Selma.

On Tuesday, once again at the Brown Chapel, 1,500 marchers, those from Selma now joined by activists from far parts of the country, heard King describe the path ahead: "There may be beatings, jailings, and tear gas. But I would rather die on the highways of Alabama than make a butchery of my conscience." Two abreast, they began walking to the Edmund Pettus Bridge. But King had no intention of leading them across it.

The day before, a federal district judge had issued an injunction against King's march to Montgomery. It presented a major problem. King had never before defied a federal court order, but ministers, expecting to march, were pouring in from all over, and the SNCC people were urging him to ignore the judge. United States attorney general Nicholas Katzenbach, by telephone from Washington, begged him not to. "Dr. King, you promised you would not," Katzenbach said repeatedly. Tugged one way by SNCC and the ministers, another by the administration, King at last

On March 9, 1965, King was among 2,000 civil rights demonstrators in Alabama who attempted for the second time in 3 days to march from Selma to Montgomery. But the protest failed once again to reach Montgomery. At the Edmund Pettus Bridge, a blockade of state troopers, backed by a court order, barred the marchers from advancing any farther.

decided to march. "Mr. Attorney General," he said, "you have not been a black man in America for three hundred years."

Alarmed by the prospect of another bloodbath, President Johnson dispatched Le Roy Collins, a former governor of Florida, to Selma as his personal emissary. He saw King and informed him the president did not want a march. Collins asked if he would consider leading the marchers to the Edmund Pettus Bridge, then return to town, provided the troopers did not interfere. Opening the door to compromise, King said he was not sure "what I can get my people to do, but if you will get Sheriff Clark and Lingo to accept something like that, I will try."

Sensing a deal, Collins located Clark and Lingo lounging about a local Pontiac dealership. They had gotten orders from Governor Wallace to avoid a repeat of Sunday's violence, and they accepted Collins's offer. "Both sides kept their word to the letter," Collins recalled. The troopers backed off, and King's people marched onto the bridge, knelt in prayer, sang "We Shall Overcome," then turned around and walked back to the Brown Chapel.

The turnaround may have preserved the peace, but it enraged SNCC. Kept in the dark about King's dealings with Collins, the SNCC workers had fully expected to battle through the troopers and attempt a march to Montgomery. The failure to do so ignited their anger. King was a coward, a traitor to the movement, some said. Back at the Brown Chapel, King only made matters worse by not leveling with the SNCC leaders about the compromise. There was no quelling their anger. With the exception of John Lewis, SNCC withdrew from the Selma campaign, thereby causing a serious rupture in the civil rights movement that would never be healed.

The night following the turnaround march, James J. Reeb, a white Unitarian minister from Boston, and two friends who had also heeded King's call to Selma ate dinner at a soul food restaurant. Afterward, walk-ing back to the Brown Chapel, they heard someone call, "Hey, you niggers!" Before they could know what was happening, four young whites in wind-breakers were on top of them, punching and clubbing. One smashed a two-by-four onto Reeb's head, crush-ing his skull. The minister fell into a coma, and two days later he died.

Reeb's death and "Bloody Sunday" speeded up the Johnson administration's plans for voting rights legislation. On the evening of March 15, 1965, Pres-ident Johnson, on prime-time television, appeared before Congress to plead for a powerful voting rights law. Johnson, not normally a rousing speaker, deliv-ered a spellbinding speech. "This time, on this issue, there must be no delay, no hesitation, and no com-promise with our purpose," he said. Blacks were seek-ing their entitlement, "the full blessings of American life," and "their cause must be our cause, too." Every person, he concluded, must work to "overcome the crippling legacy of bigotry and injustice. And . . . we shall . . . overcome."

In Selma, King and his SCLC friends watched the president stand before Congress and the nation and join their ranks. In all their years of struggle, they had never seen King cry. But when Johnson said, "We shall overcome," tears flooded his eyes and rolled down his face.

It was left for King to complete what had twice been started: the march to Montgomery. President Johnson guaranteed the necessary security by taking control of the Alabama National Guard from Wallace and ordering the guard and U.S. marshals to protect the march along Highway 80. On March 21, a bright Sunday, King and 3,200 supporters left Selma by crossing the now placid Edmund Pettus Bridge. By arrangement, most of them peeled away outside town, leaving 300 freedom marchers to make the entire four-day trek to Montgomery.

Along the way, whites came to the roadside to wave Confederate flags and to shout, "Nigger King, go home!" but the National Guard prevented them from doing anything more. The band of 300 slogged through rain and mud, inspiring hope among the long-suffering blacks of central Alabama. "What do you want?" a marcher would shout. "Freedom!" the blacks along the highway would reply.

King was with the march most of the way, leaving it for a day, then rejoining it near the end. In Montgomery, nearly 25,000 people, many of whom had traveled thousands of miles to be there, followed King up Dexter Avenue and past his old church to the gleaming white state capitol building. "This is the day! This is the day!" cried a black woman as she marched.

The throng pressed in about the capitol, where 104 years earlier Jefferson Davis had assumed the presidency of the Confederacy and where George

"We are on the move now to the land of freedom," King said in leading a third protest march from Selma to Montgomery on March 21, 1965. An executive order by President Lyndon B. Johnson called for nearly 2,000 National Guardsmen to provide security for the demonstrators during the 4-day trek.

Wallace now preached segregation. But the day of white supremacy was nearly done. In a few months, Congress would approve Johnson's voting rights bill, and in a few years, black voters would change the face of southern politics. King acknowledged their great progress:

I know you are asking today, "How long will it take?" I come to say to you this afternoon, however difficult the moment, however frustrating the hour, it will not be long, because truth pressed to the earth will rise again.

How long? Not long, because no lie can live forever.

How long? Not long, because you will reap what you sow.

How long? Not long, because the arm of the moral universe is long but it bends toward justice.

How long? Not long, because mine eyes have seen the glory of the coming of the Lord. . . . ❦

9

"WE DON'T WANT YOU HERE"

O N AUGUST 6, 1965, in the President's Room of the Capitol, Lyndon B. Johnson signed into law the forceful, uncompromising Voting Rights Act. "Today is a triumph for freedom as huge as any victory that's ever been won on any battlefield," said the president. The Voting Rights Act was the deed that ratified the civil rights movement of Martin Luther King. The southern system of segregation and legal discrimination was a dead letter.

Less than a week later, Watts, the black ghetto of Los Angeles, erupted into one of the most frightening race riots in American history. Arsonists and snipers turned southeast Los Angeles into a combat zone. Mobs roamed the neighborhood, smashing windows, looting merchandise, screaming, "Burn, baby, burn," the slogan of a local disk jockey. Eventually, 14,000 National Guardsmen entered Watts, rumbling through the streets in tanks and armored cars, trying to restore order. When the sickening violence ended, death and ruin were everywhere. The riot took

After civil rights activist James Meredith was shot on June 6, 1966, during a one-man "walk against fear" to protest white violence in Mississippi, King (front row, center) and other black leaders took over the march. Despite the urging of some of his associates to respond with black militancy, King maintained: "I'm not going to use violence, no matter who says it."

34 lives, injured more than 1,000 people, resulted in 4,000 arrests, damaged or destroyed 977 buildings, and saw $35 million worth of property go up in smoke.

King got the news about Watts while on his way to Puerto Rico for a few days' rest. The more he heard about the riot, the less he felt like a vacation. Changing his plans, he flew to Los Angeles and toured the still-smoldering ghetto. The devastation of the area shocked him, and the attitude of many residents was profoundly depressing. Some pretended not to know who he was. Others heckled him when he spoke. The prophet of nonviolence, they were saying, had nothing to offer them. A group of youngsters told him, "We won."

"How can you say you won," King asked, "when 34 Negroes are dead, your community is destroyed, and whites are using the riots as an excuse for inaction?"

"We won because we made them pay attention to us," replied a young man.

In a way, the young man was right. The Watts riot, in its horror, forced attention on the northern ghettos and coincided with a shift in the civil rights movement from South to North. Half the blacks in the United States lived outside the South, and their problems were not with laws that kept them out of lunch counters or off the voting rolls. They had long had legal equality, but all too often their life was filled with unemployment, poverty, inferior housing, broken homes, crime, and disease.

When King looked north, he became outraged by "the Negro's repellent slum life," and he decided to employ the nonviolent direct action that had succeeded in the South to a northern city. In early 1966, King and the SCLC came to Chicago. It was the logical place. With a black population greater than 1 million, the nation's second-largest city practiced every typical northern form of racial discrimination.

King and his wife, Coretta, fix up their apartment in one of Chicago's poorest black ghettos during the 1966 campaign to win civil rights for urban blacks. "If we can break the system in Chicago, it can be broken anywhere in the country," King argued at the start of what became known as the Chicago Freedom Movement.

Chicago's political, financial, and real estate interests informally, but effectively, kept the black population segregated in the ghettos on the south and west sides of town. Segregated housing led to all-black schools where the quality of education was atrocious. Living in a ghetto, going to miserable schools, most blacks had two strikes against them when it came to finding a job—and poverty, unemployment, and welfare were the sad facts of life.

King's target was ghetto housing. "Our primary objective," he said, "will be to bring about the unconditional surrender of forces dedicated to the creation and maintenance of slums and ultimately to make slums a moral and financial liability upon the whole community."

"You can't really get close to the poor without living and being there with them," King said. So instead of staying in a comfortable hotel, in late January 1966 he rented an apartment for $90 a month in the part of the West Side known as Lawndale but more often called "Slumdale." For the next nine months, on and off, he commuted between Atlanta and this miserable Chicago apartment, with flaking plaster, broken-down appliances, and cramped rooms.

The Chicago movement began slowly. King toured the ghetto, met with community leaders, and denounced the tenement landlords. But, in truth, he had no idea how to eliminate slums, nor did the SCLC have a coherent plan for Chicago. Andrew Young conceded, "We haven't gotten things under control. The strategy hasn't emerged yet, but we know what we are dealing with and eventually we'll come up with answers."

What they were dealing with was the power of Richard J. Daley, mayor of Chicago, chairman of the Cook County Democratic Organization, and known far and wide as "the last of the big city bosses." A pudgy, narrow-shouldered man, given to purple-faced rages and slips of the tongue—"Racism doesn't have a Chinaman's chance in Chicago," he once said— Daley was nevertheless as shrewd a politician as there was in America. He bossed Chicago's fabled political machine, and, far from excluding blacks from its workings, he encouraged their participation. Chicago blacks loyally trooped to the polls every election day to give Daley and the Democratic ticket impossibly large majorities. In return, they received city jobs and city favors from the mayor, as did the Irish, Italians, Poles, Czechs, Jews, and every other ethnic group that backed the machine.

What Daley could not do for blacks was assist them out of their ghettos into the more pleasant, affordable homes in all-white neighborhoods. The bedrock of Daley's machine was white. If whites saw blacks moving in next door, they would surely blame it on the mayor, and, just as surely, his political goose would be cooked.

Through the spring of 1966, Daley kept one step ahead of King. He admitted things in the slums were bad but said Chicago had plans to improve conditions and the city did not need "outsiders telling us what to do." With charts, graphs, and position papers, the mayor outlined his commitment to slum clearance, public housing, and antipoverty programs. To Lawndale, King's Chicago neighborhood, he sent an army of building inspectors who wrote up violations of the city code and forced landlords to make repairs. In face-to-face meetings, Daley respectfully deferred to King, saying he shared his goals and was doing all he could to realize them.

As the Chicago movement fizzled, King was back in the South. On June 6, 1966, James Meredith, the first black admitted to the University of Mississippi, was shot and wounded by a white assailant while on a one-man voter registration march across Mississippi. King at once decided to carry on for the fallen Meredith. For the next three weeks, the "James Meredith March Against Fear" traveled 200 miles under the scorching sun down U.S. Highway 51 from Memphis, Tennessee, to Jackson, Mississippi.

It was neither a happy nor successful demonstration. Whites along the way bullied, taunted, and abused the marchers. In Philadelphia, Mississippi—strong Klan country—a white mob interrupted King's speech by shouting and tossing cherry bombs. Afterward, the marchers' camp was strafed with rifle fire. Miraculously, no one was hurt. Long years in the South had prepared King to anticipate violence from whites, but the great disappointment of the Meredith march was division among blacks.

Civil rights activist James Meredith falls to the ground after being shot during his one-man "walk against fear." According to King, the attack on Meredith clearly demonstrated that "a reign of terror still exists in the South."

King had hoped the march would recapture the black unity of earlier days, and in Memphis he planned the demonstration with Floyd McKissick, the national director of CORE, and Stokely Carmichael, the new chairman of SNCC. But they and their organizations were increasingly militant, and it did not take long on the highway to discover not everyone liked marching at King's pace. One day, he overheard some SNCC and CORE people talking. "I'm not for that nonviolence stuff anymore," said one. "If one of these damn Mississippi crackers touches me, I'm gonna knock the hell out of him." King appreciated the whites who joined the march, but Carmichael and the SNCC wanted an all-black affair. "We don't need any more white phonies and liberals invading our movement," he said.

As the march wound its way deeper into Mississippi, Carmichael got more militant. In Greenwood, after spending a brief time in jail, he told a crowd, "I ain't going to jail no more. Every courthouse in Mississippi ought to be burned down to get rid of the dirt." Then, over and over, he shouted, "We want black power," and each time the crowd cried back, "Black Power. Black Power."

King thought the phrase "unfortunate." It sounded too much like black supremacy or black separatism, both of which he totally opposed. It also drove a wedge into the march. At rallies, the SNCC and CORE people chanted, "Black Power," while the SCLC marchers called back, "Freedom now," their longtime cry. Finally, as the march neared Jackson, King had it out with Carmichael and SNCC. "I pleaded with the group to abandon the Black Power slogan," he said later. It refused, but after a long wrangle, it agreed to stop the shouting contest with the SCLC.

The Black Power slogan quickly made Carmichael into a national figure. Before long, he was denouncing integration as "a subterfuge for the maintenance of white supremacy." In direct opposition to King, he said: "Black people should and must fight back."

King knew Black Power had strong appeal, particularly in the ghettos of the North. A day after the divided Meredith march reached its destination, he was on his way back to Chicago. There, the SCLC had to show that nonviolent direct action still worked. "We have got to deliver results—nonviolent results in a northern city—to protect the nonviolent movement," said Andrew Young.

On July 10, 1966, "Freedom Sunday," King launched his Chicago open housing drive. He declared to a crowd of 30,000 in sweltering 98-degree weather, "I do not see the answer to our problems in violence. . . . This day we must decide to fill up the jails of Chicago, if necessary, to end the slums." On Monday morning, Mayor Daley received him at City Hall, and, as before, he trotted out all of the housing and welfare programs Chicago had in the works.

Amid the blistering heat of the following day, some black youngsters near King's Lawndale apartment turned on the fire hydrants in the streets and cooled off in the gushing water. When the police

King speaks at a Mississippi voter registration drive in June 1966. At left is Stokely Carmichael, who replaced John Lewis as chairman of the Student Nonviolent Coordinating Committee (SNCC) and lobbied for blacks to take a more militant approach to gaining their rights.

arrived to close off the hydrants, it led to trouble. A few hours later, Martin and Coretta were returning from dinner, driving through the West Side. King noticed a group running along the avenue. "Those people—I wonder if there's a riot starting," he said. Indeed, there was, triggered by the hydrant episode. Over the next few days, violence gripped the West Side. Snipers appeared on the rooftops of tenements and housing projects, firing away blindly. Two blacks, one a 14-year-old girl, were killed, and incidents of arson and looting spread across several square miles.

On the worst night of the turmoil, King, Young, and the comedian Dick Gregory cruised the West Side, stopping at street corners, churches, bars, and barbecue joints. Everywhere, King pleaded for non-violence, confronting members of the area's black gangs, notorious for their violent ways, to say they should put down their guns, knives, and Molotov cocktails. He invited some back to his Lawndale apartment.

When Assistant Attorney General Roger Wilkins, President Johnson's personal representative, called on King well after midnight, he found the place "jammed with people. . . . The apartment wasn't air conditioned. There was no fan. It was not a pleasant place to be." But there was King, "this Nobel Prize laureate, sitting on the floor, having a dialogue with semiarticulate gang kids. He was holding a seminar in nonviolence, trying to convince these kids that rioting was destructive; that the way to change society was to approach it with love of yourself and of mankind and dignity in your heart."

At the end of July, the ghetto was quiet again, but, of the SCLC campaign, Young said, "We haven't found the Achilles heel of the Daley machine yet." They soon did. King announced a series of demonstrations and marches—not on the lakefront, not in the riot-scarred West Side, but in the all-white, working-class neighborhoods that excluded blacks.

The plan jolted Daley. He had lived all his life in one of these neighborhoods, and if he knew anything, he knew that blacks marching in would cause terrible trouble. The mayor was in a tight spot. If the blacks marched without police protection, a race riot was virtually certain. But if the police protected the demonstrators, infuriated whites would blame City Hall for coddling blacks. Election day was only three months away.

King did not participate in the first few marches, leaving local leaders in control. A tall, outspoken 25-year-old Chicago minister named Jesse Jackson helped guide 500 demonstrators into the all-white Gage Park neighborhood. As they approached the office of real estate firms that refused to show homes to blacks, a white crowd showered them with rocks and bottles. Jackson was hit, as the police offered scant protection. The marches continued into other neighborhoods, and residents greeted the visitors by overturning cars and screaming, "Go back to Africa. We don't want you here."

A huge rally at Soldier Field in Chicago on July 10, 1966, launched an aggressive campaign to combat housing discrimination in the city. Immediately following the demonstration, King, backed by 5,000 supporters, marched into the heart of Chicago and taped a copy of the protesters' demands to the front door of City Hall.

King is stoned by white home-owners in a Chicago suburb during an August 1966 protest march for desegregated housing. He said afterward that he had "never seen anything so hostile and so hateful as I've seen here today."

On Friday, August 5, King himself led a pilgrimage of 600 marchers, including numerous white sympathizers, into Marquette Park. This time the Chicago police were out in force. Nearly a thousand blue-helmeted cops lined the streets to shield the marchers from the white homeowners.

When King drove up, the crowd was seething, but he seemed unconcerned. "Let's get out of the car. Nothing is going to happen. These people aren't going to do anything," he said to Al Raby, a Chicago organizer. As he left his car, the police closed in around him. They could not, however, protect him from a well-aimed rock that struck him on the right temple. The blow knocked King to one knee, and the crowd roared approval, bellowing, "Nigger, go home!" and, "We want Martin Luther Coon."

Escorted and sheltered by the police, the march proceeded through the neighborhood. The whites did not let up. When it was over, King, who thought he had seen it all, was shaking his head: "I think the people from Mississippi ought to come to Chicago to learn how to hate."

Over the next two weeks, the marches continued, sometimes several a day heading to different parts of the city. Then, on August 20, King raised the stakes by unveiling plans for a march into Cicero, a Chicago suburb with 70,000 residents, none of them black. "Jesus, they won't make it," said a Cicero politician. "If they get in, they won't get out." In 1951, a horrible riot had forced out a black who tried to buy a house there, and no one thought things would be any different in 1966.

The prospect of a march into Cicero was too much for Daley. Already, the white neighborhoods were up in arms about his police protecting blacks, and more marches, with more bloodshed, threatened the health of his political organization. He decided, for the moment, to let King have what he wanted. On August 26, the city agreed that all its agencies would uphold the principles of fair housing and would work to integrate all-white neighborhoods.

King hailed the agreement. Back in Atlanta, he explained to his congregation at Ebenezer that the Chicago accord was "the most significant and far-reaching victory that has ever come about in a northern community on the whole question of open housing."

It also was not worth the paper it was written on. For Daley, it made no difference what he agreed to as long as it got King out of town. With him back in Atlanta and the Chicago movement leaderless, the mayor simply forgot about the agreement and went back to business as usual.

But in March 1967, King was back in Chicago, once more leading a march, once more delivering an impassioned speech. This time, however, it was not a renewed drive for open housing. For the first time in his life, King was marching to protest a war—the American war in Vietnam.

On February 6, 1968, King and other clergymen joined forces with 2,500 supporters at the Tomb of the Unknown Soldier in Arlington National Cemetery for a demonstration against the Vietnam War. King said of his decision to take a public stand on the war, "I could no longer remain silent about an issue that was destroying the soul of our nation."

For several years, King had been watching with alarm the deepening American commitment to the anticommunist government of South Vietnam. In the spring and summer of 1965, as President Johnson ordered intense bombing raids of the enemy and deployed tens of thousands of American combat troops in Southeast Asia, King had spoken out. He declared, "The war in Vietnam must be stopped. There must be a negotiated settlement." Finding no encouragement for an antiwar position from other black leaders, King, for the best part of two years, kept his concerns about the war to himself.

By early 1967, he was quiet no longer. By then, a quarter million American soldiers were in Vietnam, and peace seemed nowhere in sight. Breaking his silence in Los Angeles, King referred to Vietnam as "one of history's most cruel and senseless wars." In Chicago, he said the nation's war policies left America "standing before the world gutted by our own barbarity." And on April 4, at the Riverside Church in New York City, he delivered his mightiest assault: "I knew that I could never again raise my voice against the oppressed in the ghettos without having first spoken clearly to the greatest purveyor of violence in the world today—my own government."

King's words placed him in the front rank of the peace movement. Yet in 1967, opposition to the war, while growing, was seen in some quarters as bordering on treason. After the Riverside Church address, a *Life* magazine editorial declared that by connecting "civil rights with a proposal that amounts to abject surrender in Vietnam . . . King comes close to betraying the cause for which he has worked so long." Within the civil rights movement itself, some felt the same way, and Roy Wilkins, A. Philip Randolph, and Bayard Rustin all distanced themselves from King's remarks.

Nineteen sixty-seven was a year during which nonviolence seemed to fail everywhere. In Vietnam, the war escalated and expanded. And at home, the ghettos exploded. During 5 days in July, 26 died in riots in Newark, New Jersey. Disturbances rocked Milwaukee, Rochester, Tampa, and Cincinnati. In Detroit, the worst race riot in half a century left 43 dead, 2,000 injured, and 4,000 fires burning. "There were dark days before," King muttered to Stanley Levison, "but this is the darkest." That summer, Coretta said, her husband's depression "was greater than I had ever seen it before." He would tell her, "People expect me to have answers and I don't have any answers. I don't feel like speaking to people. I don't have anything to tell them."

King would not surrender. Late in 1967, he developed the idea of an SCLC-sponsored Poor People's March on Washington. By bringing thousands of the impoverished to the nation's capital, the need for economic justice would be made plain. If they built a poor people's city of shacks and tents in sight of the Capitol, perhaps Congress would see the necessity of ending poverty. As he toured the nation, he talked not only of combating poverty and ending the war but of saving the American soul.

"We're going to build our shanties right in Washington and live right there," King would cry. "I'm not playing about this thing. I've agonized over it, and I'm trying to save America. And that's what you are trying to do if you will join this movement. We're trying to save this nation! We can't continue to live in a nation every summer going up in flames, every day killing our people in Vietnam like we're killing. We can't *continue* this way as a nation and survive."

The planning for the march did not go well. By spring 1968, things were far behind schedule. Then the striking garbage collectors of Memphis, Tennessee, asked for King's help, and he answered their plea. **◆**

10

APRIL 4, 1968

FEW THINGS IMPROVED King's mood like a good response to one of his speeches, and at Mason Temple in Memphis on April 3, 1968, the small rally cheered and cheered his address. As the SCLC people drove off to a late dinner, King seemed "happy and relaxed," according to Ralph Abernathy. Long after midnight, when the 39-year-old minister returned to the Lorraine Motel, there was a nice surprise. His brother, A. D., and several friends had driven in from Louisville. They all talked and joked for hours, not turning in until shortly before dawn.

Around noon on Thursday, April 4, Abernathy nudged his old friend. "Come on now, it's time to get up." Struggling to open his eyes, King nodded but stayed where he was. "You know, we can't win this nonviolent revolution in bed," Abernathy chided.

Soon, King was awake and dressed and meeting with various people, organizing down to the last detail Monday's march supporting the garbage collectors. As they worked, they considered all the things that could go wrong, and Abernathy thought King was "grim and businesslike." Another participant said he seemed "terribly depressed. He had a great deal of anxiety."

National Guardsmen were called into Memphis, Tennessee, to monitor a civil rights demonstration on March 29, 1968, the day after a protest march led by King had dissolved into turmoil. "Maybe we just have to admit that the day of violence is here," King said after the riot took place, "and maybe we have to just give up and let violence take its course."

But King lightened up. When Andrew Young came in, King scolded him for some mistake, and, Young remembered, "He picked up a pillow and threw it at me. And I threw it back, and we ended up with five or six of us in a pillow fight." Having his brother around also pleased King. In the afternoon, from A. D.'s room, they called their mother in Atlanta, at first disguising their voices, pretending to be each other. For almost an hour, they teased, joked, and chatted.

At five, King and Abernathy walked upstairs to their shared room and got ready for dinner. King shaved, as always using a foul-smelling product called Magic Shave to protect his sensitive skin, then splashing on generous amounts of Aramis cologne. Downstairs, in the motel's courtyard, a large chauffeured Cadillac pulled up. It was the car a Memphis funeral director had loaned King, and this evening it would be delivering everyone to a dinner at the home of Samuel B. Kyles, a local minister. Later, there would be another mass meeting, and King would speak.

Kyles entered room 306 and found King rummaging through his belongings. "Somebody on the staff took my tie," he said.

"Martin, why don't you just look down at that chair?" said Abernathy.

"Oh. I thought somebody took it on me." Knotting the black-and-gold striped tie, King turned to Kyles. "I think your wife is too young to cook soul food for us. She's only thirty-one, isn't she? How can she cook soul food at that age?"

"That's right," said Abernathy. "We don't want to come over to your house and get filet mignon. We want greens, soul food—does Gwen know how to cook soul food?"

"Don't you worry," Kyles assured them.

"This shirt is too tight," King complained.

April 4, 1968, 6:00 P.M.: A mortally wounded King lies on the balcony of the Lorraine Motel in Memphis, Tennessee, while his colleagues point to the rooming house from which James Earl Ray fired the fatal shot.

"You mean you're getting too fat," Abernathy laughed. "That's the shirt I washed for you."

"It's too tight." Making the best of it, King slipped on his jacket. "Okay, let's go eat. I sure hope you're not kidding us about Gwen."

The three men walked to the balcony, but Abernathy retreated to the room to put on some after-shave. Kyles and King waited. Downstairs in the parking lot, the other SCLC staffers stood around the big

Thousands of mourners follow the farm wagon that carried King's coffin through the streets of his hometown, Atlanta, on April 9, 1968. The wagon and mules were symbols of the Poor People's Campaign, the civil rights leader's attempt to call attention to the plight of the nation's poor.

white Cadillac. The car's driver called out that King should bring a topcoat; it was getting chilly. "Okay," King replied, and he asked Abernathy to fetch it.

It was six o'clock.

Kyles started downstairs. King glanced down and noticed Ben Branch, a Chicago musician, standing with Jesse Jackson. "Ben, make sure you play 'Precious Lord, Take My Hand' at the meeting tonight," he said. "Sing it *real* pretty."

Across the street, in the bathroom window of a cheap rooming house, James Earl Ray, a black-hating drifter, aimed his .30-06 rifle at the stocky black man on the balcony of the Lorraine Motel. He had a clean shot, and he fired.

It sounded like a firecracker or a car's backfire. From the door of their room, Abernathy saw King's body sprawled on the balcony. He rushed out, bent down, and saw a huge red wound on King's right jaw. He patted him on the cheek: "Martin, Martin, this is Ralph. Do you hear me? This is Ralph." King's lips seemed to move, but he did not speak.

An hour later, in a Memphis hospital, Martin Luther King, Jr., was pronounced dead at the age of 39.

His body was returned to Atlanta, and his funeral was held at the Ebenezer Baptist Church on April 9, 1968. An impressive number of prominent people—politicians and entertainers, public servants and civil rights activists—sat quietly in the congregation. Abernathy told the grief-stricken assembly, "We gather here this morning in one of the darkest hours in the history of the black people of this nation, in one of the darkest hours in the history of all mankind."

Outside, nearly 100,000 mourners surrounded the church. Mostly, they were humble and poor and black. Yet it was they—"the battered, the scarred, and the defeated," King called them—who possessed the courage and the love that had inspired him to greatness. ❦

Coretta Scott King comforts her youngest daughter, Bernice, during funeral services for the slain civil rights leader at the Ebenezer Baptist Church in Atlanta.

APPENDIX

THE WRITINGS OF MARTIN LUTHER KING, JR.

Listed below are the books written by Martin Luther King, Jr. In addition to these works, he also wrote 60 articles that have appeared in such magazines and newspapers as *Ebony*, *The Nation*, and the *New York Times*. Many of these pieces have been reprinted in *A Testament of Hope: The Essential Writings of Martin Luther King, Jr.*, James M. Washington, ed. (New York: Harper & Row, 1986). Portions of King's writings have also been collected in *A Martin Luther King Treasury*, Alfred E. Cain, ed. (The Negro Heritage Library, Yonkers, New York: Educational Heritage, Inc., 1964).

The Measure of a Man. Philadelphia: Christian Education Press, 1959.

Strength to Love. New York: Harper & Row, 1963.

Stride Toward Freedom: The Montgomery Story. New York: Harper & Brothers, 1958.

The Trumpet of Conscience. New York: Harper & Row, 1968.

Where Do We Go from Here: Chaos or Community? New York: Harper & Row, 1967.

Why We Can't Wait. New York: New American Library, 1964.

CHRONOLOGY

1929 Born Martin Luther King, Jr., on January 15 in Atlanta, Georgia

1948 Graduates from Morehouse College; ordained as a Baptist minister

1951 Graduates from Crozer Theological Seminary

1953 Marries Coretta Scott

1954 Becomes pastor at Dexter Avenue Baptist Church in Montgomery, Alabama

1955 Receives Ph.D. degree in Systematic Theology from Boston University; joins the Montgomery bus boycott; becomes president of the Montgomery Improvement Association; first child, Yolanda, is born

1957 King founds the Southern Christian Leadership Conference (SCLC); organizes the Prayer Pilgrimage for Freedom; awarded the Spingarn Medal; second child, Martin Luther III, is born

1958 King stabbed in New York City

1959 Travels to India

1960 Becomes co-pastor at the Ebenezer Baptist Church in Atlanta; imprisoned at Reidsville state penitentiary in Georgia

1961 Launches desegregation campaign in Albany, Georgia; third child, Dexter, is born

1962 King joins racial protests in Birmingham, Alabama

1963 Arrested at a demonstration in Birmingham; writes "Letter from Birmingham Jail"; delivers "I Have a Dream" speech at the March on Washington; fourth child, Bernice, is born

1964 King awarded the Nobel Peace Prize

1965 Joins the SCLC in Selma, Alabama, for its march to Montgomery

1966 Launches the Chicago Freedom Movement; organizes the "James Meredith March Against Fear"

1967 Forms the Poor People's Campaign

1968 Assassinated on April 4 in Memphis, Tennessee

FURTHER READING

Bishop, Jim. *The Days of Martin Luther King, Jr.* New York: Putnam, 1971.

Branch, Taylor. *Parting the Waters: America in the King Years 1954–63.* New York: Simon & Schuster, 1988.

Garrow, David J. *Bearing the Cross: Martin Luther King, Jr., and the Southern Christian Leadership Conference.* New York: Morrow, 1986.

———. *The FBI and Martin Luther King, Jr.: From "Solo" to Memphis.* New York: Norton, 1981.

King, Coretta Scott. *My Life with Martin Luther King, Jr.* New York: Holt, Rinehart & Winston, 1969.

King, Martin Luther, Sr. *Daddy King: An Autobiography.* New York: Morrow, 1980.

Lewis, David L. *King: A Critical Biography.* New York: Praeger, 1970.

Lincoln, C. Eric, ed. *Martin Luther King, Jr.: A Profile.* Rev. ed. New York: Hill & Wang, 1984.

Oates, Stephen B. *Let the Trumpet Sound: The Life of Martin Luther King, Jr.* New York: Harper and Row, 1982.

Raines, Howell. *My Soul Is Rested: Movement Days in the Deep South Remembered.* New York: Putnam, 1977.

Williams, Juan. *Eyes on the Prize: America's Civil Rights Years 1954–1965.* New York: Viking Penguin, 1987.

Wofford, Harris. *Of Kennedys and Kings.* New York: Farrar, Straus & Giroux, 1980.

INDEX

PICTURE CREDITS

———•◊•———

ROBERT JAKOUBEK holds degrees in history from Indiana University and Columbia University. He is coauthor of *These United States*, an American history textbook published by Houghton Mifflin. He is also the author of *Adam Clayton Powell, Jr.*, in Chelsea House's BLACK AMERICANS OF ACHIEVEMENT series and *Harriet Beecher Stowe* in its AMERICAN WOMEN OF ACHIEVEMENT series.

NATHAN IRVIN HUGGINS is W.E.B. Du Bois Professor of History and Director of the W.E.B. Du Bois Institute for Afro-American Research at Harvard University. He previously taught at Columbia University. Professor Huggins is the author of numerous books, including *Black Odyssey: The Afro-American Ordeal in Slavery, The* *Slave and Citizen: The Life of Fred-*